S0-ALJ-101

Selling Skills For CPAs: How To Bring In New Business

Selling Skills For CPAs: How To Bring In New Business

Charles Goldsmith
Coordinator of Management Development
Deloitte, Haskins & Sells

McGraw-Hill Book Company

New York   St. Louis   San Francisco   Auckland
Bogotá   Hamburg   Johannesburg London
Madrid   Mexico   Montreal   New Delhi
Panama   Paris   São Paulo   Singapore
Sydney   Tokyo   Toronto

Library of Congress Cataloging in Publication Data

Goldsmith, Charles.
  Selling skills for CPAs: how to bring in new business.

  Includes index.
  1. Accounting—Marketing.   I. Title.   II. Title: Selling skills
for CPAs: how to bring in new business.
HF5657.G63   1985   657'.068'8   84-19382
ISBN 0-07-023671-2

  234567890 DOC/DOC 898765

ISBN 0-07-023671-2

The editors for this book were Martha Jewett and Jim Bessent,
the designer was Dennis Sharkey, and the production
supervisor was Thomas G. Kowalczyk. It was set in Palatino
by Achorn Graphics.

Printed and bound by R. R. Donnelley.

Contents

Chapter 5
Preparing for the Sales Meeting   *57*

Chapter 6
Starting the Meeting   *77*

Chapter 7
Identifying the Prospect's Real Needs   *85*

Chapter 8
Presenting Your Firm's Capability   *97*

Preface

The Need to Sell in a Competitive Environment

The late 1970s ushered in a period of fierce competition for the accounting profession. Spurred by a relaxation of their own standards on advertising and solicitation, antimonopolistic rumblings by the federal government, and the demands of a more sophisticated client, accounting firms found themselves for the first time in the position not only of fighting for new clients but also of defending their existing client base from other firms. It was clearly a time of change. For many in the profession it was, to put it mildly, difficult. Yet CPAs began to recognize the need to actively sell their services. Firms that had previously maintained a gentleman's agreement to stay away from each other's clients and had looked with disdain at the very thought of soliciting clients were now hiring marketing directors, developing marketing plans, and urging their people to "get out there and sell."

It was this dynamic environment and my numerous years of selling and training salespeople that prompted me to learn more about how CPAs would adapt to this new role. I started by selecting this subject as the topic of my doctoral dissertation, "A Descriptive Profile of the Experiences, Attitudes and Behavior of Certified Public Accountants Who Successfully Sell Financial Services." In the course of my study I interviewed a large number of accountants and consultants who were successful in selling their services. Their experiences and the experiences of thousands of other professional salespeople I have worked with became the raw material for this book. I analyzed this material, compared it to the state of the art of selling, and designed what I believe is a book that is tailored to the specific needs of those in the accounting profession.

Buying and Selling Accounting Services

While this is a book about selling accounting services, it is just as much a book about buying these services. As any successful salesperson knows, it is the buyer who decides when a sale takes place. And this happens when prospective clients are reasonably convinced that the service they will receive has value equal to the fee they are asked to pay. Therefore the book devotes considerable space to exploring the special needs and motivations of prospective clients.

It is also an intensive guide to effective one-on-one communication between the CPA seller and the prospective client. One may develop strategic marketing plans, produce attractive brochures, and place attention-getting advertisements. But nothing happens until the buyer and the seller sit down, talk to each other, understand each other, and build trust with each other. Only at that point can agreement take place. Therefore, much of this book deals with hearing what a prospect says, understanding what it means, and responding in a way that brings the buyer and seller closer together. In this respect a good portion of the book is devoted to providing answers to the large number of troublesome objections that a prospect may raise.

Prospects follow a certain thinking process in arriving at a decision to buy. It is not rigid, but it can be reasonably anticipated by the CPA seller. Much like following a map to find the right direction in taking a trip, the CPA must know where the prospect is in the buying process; this dictates the selling strategy. This book follows a logical but flexible sequence of steps from the time of initial contact to the close of the sale.

Acknowledgments

I owe much to my wife Yvonne, who added a client's point of view, edited every word of the text, and stoked my sometimes flagging energy. In the process we sacrificed a few of our favorite activities: seeing the latest movie, bike riding in Central Park, and visiting with friends. I also appreciate the critical review given by David Powell, partner in charge of my department, and finally, I am indebted to the partners of Deloitte, Haskins & Sells, who contributed so much to the content of this book.

Charles Goldsmith

Selling Skills For CPAs: How To Bring In New Business

Introduction

"Bill, what the hell went wrong? I thought you said you were confident we'd get Rollins as a client!"

The senior partner's expression was puzzled and his manner visibly disturbed. Bill was uncomfortable, not only because of George's uncharacteristic outburst but also because he had a sense of failure, a feeling that, as a CPA firm partner, he did not experience often. Bill got through the rest of the meeting somehow, but his attention was not really on the other matters being discussed.

As Bill returned to his office, his thoughts kept reviewing the events of the last several months and his handling of the Rollins situation. What *had* gone wrong? How had he allowed the firm's strongest competitor in the city to snatch a substantial fee right out of his hand?

Bill had met Fred Rollins about a year ago at a Rotary Club meeting. Fred was the outgoing, down-to-earth type, an entrepreneur who had opened the doors of his computer software company 8 years ago.

Coupling his knowledge and drive with the fast growth of the industry, Fred had turned his dream into a $20 million company, and the future looked even brighter. Fred and Bill hit it off from the start and found several areas of common interest, and they began to play golf together fairly regularly. Their wives also got along well, and the two couples enjoyed getting together for dinner every month or so.

From time to time, usually following the golf game, Fred would discuss certain aspects of his business. Despite explosive growth, Rollins's company was having problems; profits were not keeping pace with sales. Fred complained that he had to make every business decision himself, and like most people, he was sure he was paying too much in taxes.

It became apparent that Fred's business was maturing rapidly and that he needed good business and personal financial advice. It was clear also that Fred's needs were not being satisfied by his present accounting firm.

Fred began to look very much like a viable client. He knew of Bill's firm and had commented more than once about its fine reputation. This pleased Bill because he had a lot of pride in his firm, a pride that had its inception at the time he joined the firm right out of college 15 years ago. From time to time, he discussed the firm's various services with Fred and emphasized their innovative approach to efficient auditing. Fred would listen, nod approvingly, and ask an occasional question.

Bill's confidence grew with each meeting. He felt it was just a matter of time before Fred would recognize that he needed a firm like Bill's, and because of their good personal relationship, it should be relatively easy to discuss the possibility and come to agreement. And now this.

Bill had to admit he really couldn't answer George's question. What had gone wrong? Did he know Fred as well as he thought he did or, more specifically, did he know what Fred really wanted from his business? Did he know enough about Fred's business? Had he failed to hit the real issues? Bill had tried to present his firm's accounting and auditing services in a clear and logical manner, but now that he thought about it, Fred's reaction had been more polite than interested. Bill wondered . . . had he conveyed the excitement that he felt about his firm or had he come on with that calm detached manner that worked so well in solving client problems? Furthermore, Bill could not recall any objections Fred raised to changing accountants, but, then again, he had not tried to probe for any objections. Bill had to admit that he never once asked Fred for his business; he had just assumed that Fred would come to him. He had taken Fred for granted; he saw that clearly. But if he had another chance, what would he do differently? And how would he go about it?

* * *

More and more small and large CPA firms throughout the United States and other countries are experiencing scenarios similar to this one. Sometimes there is a happier ending. Success or failure in a specific instance notwithstanding, how new clients are obtained is rapidly changing, and certified public accountants (CPAs) increasingly are finding themselves in unfamiliar and often uncomfortable selling situations, very unlike the "good old days" when clients practically walked in the door. Let's take a closer look at what has happened.

Traditionally, public accounting firms have taken a relatively passive approach to acquiring new business. In general, clients were attained through personal relationships or from recommendations of bankers, lawyers, or satisfied clients. Often, the accounting firm's reputation for technical expertise was its most effective sales technique.

More recently, for a variety of reasons, accounting firms find that the traditional methods of bringing in business are not as effective. One reason is that fewer clients today are in awe of the professional's credentials. Client executives are more sophisticated in selecting and using accounting firms, and they do not hesitate to replace one accounting firm with another if the first firm's services are not satisfactory. They expect client-centered performance in addition to good technical services.

Also, accounting firms have become more competitive. Sometimes, several compete for the same engagement. Some firms are willing to perform work at a significant discount, further sharpening competition among the firms.

Additionally, the United States government has taken exception to that portion of the profession's code of ethics which deals with restrictions on direct solicitation and advertising. Following the U.S. Supreme Court's ruling that such restrictions result in restraint of trade, in 1978 the profession relaxed its rules on both advertising and solicitation.

In the international market, accounting firms are beginning to recognize the competitive requirements for acquiring and retaining clients. Until now, much of the overseas accountant's task was to audit subsidiary companies of major U.S. corporations, basically a passive role. Now, growing feelings of nationalism and the aggressive growth plans of foreign companies are motivating overseas accountants to search out business opportunities within their own countries.

Thus, increased competition, new government regulations, and changing attitudes within the accounting profession constitute a new environment for firms offering financial services. Success in this new environment suggests, even mandates, a significant change in the CPA firm's traditional "you call us" approach to the marketplace. CPAs find for the first time the need to sell their services aggressively. The economic implications are fairly obvious. Firms that do not become more aggressive marketers stand to lose both revenue and their relative position in the profession. This includes local or individual practitioners, who will not only find it more difficult to acquire new clients but may also see their carefully built practices erode.

Some accounting firms are responding to the new environment by adopting marketing concepts and activities that are similar to those employed by their clients. Public relations, advertising, and selling represent some of the activities that fall under the marketing umbrella. Personal selling, in particular, is the responsibility of every accountant/consultant. Without an effective personal selling effort, there is no new business.

Unfortunately, most accountants are not prepared by education or by experience to successfully perform the selling role. They never were taught how to sell, nor were they told when they joined the firm that selling would eventually be one of their responsibilities. To some CPAs, the idea of selling is uncomfortable and even frightening. One CPA firm partner observed about his peers: "They're scared to death; they're afraid they'll fail."

Other accountants, like George and Bill, after encountering a situation such as our opening scenario, recognize the need to respond to changing conditions and to approach the selling role with a positive attitude. But, a positive attitude is not enough. As with any new skill, basic techniques must be learned and put into practice.

This book deals exclusively with the personal selling of accounting and related services. Other marketing activities of a firm, such as research, advertising, and public relations, cannot be adequately covered in the space planned for this book. Also, and perhaps more important, these activities are usually directed by a few senior partners or outside consultants, and most of the members of an accounting firm are not involved. But almost everyone in the firm has the opportunity to sell. True, some are more interested in selling than others, and some do it better, but from the new staff accountant right out of school who is building contacts for future business to the senior partner who is closing the sale on a Fortune 500 company, everyone can get involved in the selling experience. A firm can spend a great deal of time and money with the other marketing activities, but eventually, a buyer and a seller wind up sitting down and talking to each other, trying to determine if the needs of the first can be satisfactorily met by the second.

This book is designed to help you in two ways: (1) to understand the concepts and skills of successful selling and (2) to gain the confidence and motivation to get out and do it! You will receive specific guidelines and techniques for conducting a successful sales effort from the time you first plan to meet a prospect through the final step of closing the sale with a new client.

Many of the insights and strategies developed in this book come from interviews that were held with CPAs and consultants who are highly successful in selling financial services. Their experiences are related in their own words and offer practical suggestions for tackling the selling challenges that lie ahead. Therefore, you will want to pay particular attention to the quotes that are given in each chapter.

Throughout the book, the words "prospect" and "buyer" are used to identify or describe a potential client—one who can benefit from your services. Because of the usual one-on-one nature of the selling relationship, the singular expression is used more often than the plural.

The first two chapters of this book briefly examine how selling professional services is like and unlike selling other services and products; what the selling environment is like, to show you what you are getting into; and how other CPAs feel about their new role. Then we will get into the heart of the book, with each succeeding chapter discussing and demonstrating a specific step in the selling process. The final chapter examines the personal qualities that are needed to give you "the edge" and offers some ways to develop these qualities.

Chapters 3 through 12 conclude with skill-building techniques, which ask you to practice with an actual prospect some of the skills covered in the chapter. These practical exercises follow the selling process step by step and will help you to quickly become more proficient in your selling skills. Do them. I know of no better way to get started toward results.

Chapter One

Selling Professional Services

Many professionals, including CPAs, attorneys, doctors, engineers, etc., have admitted to a lack of knowledge about marketing and selling. They may have taken the equivalent of Marketing 101 in college or had some personal selling experience as a youth, but for the most part, they have limited understanding about a subject that has suddenly emerged as a major responsibility. That limitation can inhibit even getting started, much less succeeding. One CPA describes the feeling:

After years of experience in a field I was very comfortable with and was generally considered to be, if not an expert, at least a very knowledgeable person, I suddenly found myself having to understand and put into practice this whole new skill of selling our services. And I was supposed to produce right away! Talk about a sobering and frightening experience. The only consolation I had was that most of my partners felt the same way.

This chapter does not present detailed information about marketing or selling, but rather it clarifies some basic questions: What activities are included under marketing? How does selling fit into marketing? How do selling tangible products and selling intangible services differ? What are the special qualities of selling professional services?

THE MARKETING UMBRELLA

A number of activities are included under the marketing umbrella, for example, market research, targeting prospects or industries, advertising, public relations and publicity, sales promotion, direct mail, brochures, seminars, alumni relations, trade shows, political activities, industrial specialization, and personal selling. And there are probably more.

Each activity has a specific purpose and may be used effectively by an accounting firm or single practitioner. A number of books describe these activities in more detail and give advice about how they can be implemented.

Generally, advertising, publicity, mailings, brochures, and similar marketing techniques reach a wide audience but with minimal impact. They compete for the reader's attention with everything else that was in the newspaper that day or with every piece of junk mail that came in and passed quickly into the wastebasket. However, seminars, alumni relations, and other more personal selling activities aim at a much smaller audience but carry a far greater impact. It is like the difference between a shotgun and a rifle—one gives coverage, the other impact. Again, each has its purpose, and the specific strategy of the firm should dictate which activities receive its emphasis, time, effort, and resources.

Personal selling is the most highly focused of the marketing activities and has the potential for making the greatest impact on a prospect. There are similarities and differences between the selling of products and the selling of services, and selling professional services has its own special qualities.

SELLING PRODUCTS

A consumer goods company puts millions of dollars into an advertising and sales promotion campaign to sell a new low-priced home product, say, a detergent. Buyers who perceive a need for the product and know what it is supposed to do will be stimulated to search it out at the nearest supermarket. There, they make a decision to buy or not to buy the detergent. In some cases, a salesperson will assist in the buying decision by answering questions or pointing out certain advantages of the product. But usually, the customer will make the decision to buy without help, based on previous knowledge and experience with a similar product. Furthermore, this decision will be aided because the customer can see and touch the product. This is a particular quality of products—they can be seen, touched, tasted, heard and smelled, which creates a familiar and often reliable basis for making a decision to buy or not to buy.

In this situation, the product, with the help of the advertising and sales promotion campaign, was brought to the attention of the customers. From that point the product pretty much sold itself, primarily because the buyers knew what they wanted and understood what the product could do. As long as the price was right, there was no reason to delay the purchase. In this case, the personal selling activity was absent or minimal.

However, as a product becomes more sophisticated and expensive and we are less sure of our needs and the ability of the product to fill those needs, we depend more on the knowledge and experience of the salesperson. For example, many people who are buying or thinking of buying a home computer are not sure exactly how to use it or which computer is best for them. They may depend on the knowledge and experience of the salesperson to provide answers about the right hardware and software.

Interestingly, accounting firms are now beginning to offer specific products such as financial planning packages to their clients and prospective clients. These products are still somewhat intangible compared to our previous examples. Still, it is a step toward the development and marketing of products, something accountants could never have foreseen a few years ago.

SELLING SERVICES

Although there are many similarities between selling products and selling services, there are also differences. For example, unlike a product, a service is intangible. You may observe it when it is occurring or evaluate it when it is finished, but before you buy it you are pretty much working in the dark. You cannot use your five senses to help you determine if that service is going to satisfy you or solve your problem. Let's look at another example.

You want to have the windows in your house or apartment washed. You hear about one service which is supposed to do a good job. You can't very well ask for a demonstration, so based on what you know about them, and a little trust, you retain their services. For $60 or $70, depending on the number of windows you have, you either get a good job or something less than that. If it is a poor job, the worst that can happen is that you're out a few bucks and you need to find a new window washing service.

Now, let's take a more serious case. Your new sports car isn't working too well. In fact, it's performing worse than your 7-year-old clunker that you drive to the train station each day. You need to have your $20,000 work of art examined and fixed by a service station that knows what it's doing. But how do you evaluate service? What are they going to do to your dream car? Will they return it to its former matchless performance? Sure, your friend recommended someone who did a good job on his car. Unfortunately, there is no way you will unquestionably know the result on yours because you can't evaluate their service with your usually reliable physical senses. You'll contact a couple of the better-known stations, try to evaluate their competence, and eventually, with some comfort in a promised warranty, you'll turn your car over to a couple of mechanics with grease-smeared overalls who view your pride and joy as the pile of metal, rubber, and fabric it really is. A few days later they tell you that they know what the problem is and give you an estimate that equals the current value of the train station clunker. After an agonizing moment of reflection, you work up your courage and tell them to go ahead. After all, your car is going to be smoothly purring again, isn't it?

In making your decision, you again placed trust in a couple of mechanics whose service you could not evaluate until the job was finished. Only this time your risk was greater than it was with the window washers. Here's an axiom about the risk-trust relationship: the greater the risk to the buyer, the greater the amount of trust placed in the seller. To put it another way, for emphasis: the more you have to lose, the more you need to trust the person you're dealing with. We'll talk more about trust and risk later in the chapter, but now let's move on to the selling of professional services.

SELLING PROFESSIONAL SERVICES

The beginning of this chapter identified the principal marketing activities and pointed out that advertising, direct mail, and other nonpersonal marketing functions are most effective when they sell tangible, low-cost products that are understood by the consumer and can be evaluated through the five senses. It became clear that costlier, more sophisticated products demanded a stronger and better selling effort by the salesperson. Then we saw how selling services is strongly influenced by the reputation of the seller, the seller's knowledge of the buyer's problem, and how the buyer personally feels about the seller. We also saw how the elements of trust become increasingly important as the buyer's risk situation increases. In selling professional services, we reach the highest degree of risk and thus the greatest need for trust by the buyer.

Professional services are provided by people with extensive and special training, such as physicians, attorneys, bankers, engineers, and CPAs. The exact application of the particular service varies depending on the specific needs of the buyer or client. Often, the need is of vital interest to the client, as in the patient-physician relationship.

Until the mid-1960s, little was written about exactly what a professional had to offer in the way of services and how that differed from products and other types of services. Then Warren Wittreich, in a *Harvard Business Review* article, outlined what he believed to be the basic concepts which contribute to the successful selling of professional services. These concepts are minimizing uncertainty, understanding problems, and buying the professional.[1]

Minimizing uncertainty. A professional service must make a direct contribution to the *reduction of the uncertainties* involved in managing a business. The proper assessment of a service, unlike tangible goods, usually must take into account the impact of its performance on the client's business.

Hence, the seller of professional services is offering the buyer not only skills and resources but also a sense of confidence, reduction of doubt, easing of risk, or simply peace of mind.

Understanding problems. A professional service must come directly to grips with a fundamental problem of the business purchasing that service. The successful performance of the service, far more so than the successful production of a product, depends on an understanding of the client's business.

---

[1] Warren J. Wittreich, "How to Buy/Sell Professional Services," *Harvard Business Review*, vol. 44, no. 2, 1966, p. 128.

Ideally, the client can identify and explain the business problem to the professional, who then provides the correct solution. Realistically, this situation occurs only infrequently. More often, the client has only a vague idea of what the real problem is. That is why doctors, attorneys, accountants, and other professionals will spend considerable time diagnosing a problem before providing the answer.

Buying the professional. A professional service can only be purchased meaningfully from someone *who is capable of rendering the service.* Selling ability and personality by themselves are meaningless.

In a company that manufactures products, the product is usually designed by one group, manufactured by another, sold by a third group, and serviced by a fourth group. As long as the product does what it is supposed to do in a satisfactory manner, the buyer does not care about the separate responsibilities of the various groups.

In professional services, the responsibility rests with the professionals, who are expected to personally produce what they promise. A patient going in for serious surgery expects that the operation will be performed by the surgeon who advised; the defendant in court expects to be represented by the attorney who accepted the case. Similarly, the client of accounting services expects to receive the attention and expertise of the person who sold the services. Although certain duties in every profession can be delegated, for the most part, the buyer/client/patient expects to get the personal attention of the professional with whom a contact or agreement was made.

Understanding these special characteristics of selling professional services is important to professionals who are new to selling. They are often confused and disturbed about their selling role because they believe it must be patterned after the hard sell image of the stereotypical professional salesperson.

An interesting distinction between the professional salesperson and the professional who sells is made by Aubrey Wilson in his book, *The Marketing of Professional Services.*[2] Wilson believes that professional salespeople see themselves primarily as individuals with an outstanding ability to sell virtually anything. Perceiving their role as limited to selling, the personal qualities that count are those of a salesperson. The services of others in their company are called on to handle substantive problems. The professional salesperson of breakfast cereals,

---

[2]Aubrey Wilson, *The Marketing of Professional Services*, McGraw-Hill, New York, 1972, pp. 29–31.

ball bearings, or automobiles sells energetically, aggressively, and on tangible considerations. When forced into an intangible selling situation, the professional salesperson may adopt a rigid set of sales techniques that just don't work.

In contrast, says Wilson, professionals who also possess sales ability perceive themselves first and foremost wholly competent in and committed to their profession. The ability to identify and isolate key factors of a problem provide the professional's main business, intellectual interest, and job satisfaction. Even sometimes to the detriment of the overall selling activity, professionals become personally involved in the problem solving, knowing either by training or through experience that they must demonstrate a personal competence equal to that of their prospects. This is particularly true for those CPAs who are successful in personal selling.

PERSONAL SELLING FOR CPAS

Personal selling in the accounting field has a role in three distinct marketing opportunities. The first is practice retention, that is, retaining clients one already has. Because of increased competition for clients and their growing sophistication, a firm can no longer assume that it can keep a client indefinitely. An existing client cannot be taken for granted; rather, one must "sell" that client every day as if he were a new prospect.

Second, additional services may be sold to existing clients. For example, a tax client may become an audit client, or the auditor may see opportunities to bring in the firm's management services to help the client establish a cost system. The ability to expand services to existing clients assumes that a need which is unfulfilled in an existing client has been identified and that, based on previous good experience with the accounting firm, the client believes the need can be fulfilled by the firm.

The third selling opportunity, usually considered the most challenging, is acquiring new clients. Knowing relatively little at first about the new prospect, the accountant must wrestle the prospect away from her present accountant. Often there are other accounting firms competing for the same new client. Because of these challenges, selling new clients can provide the greatest personal satisfaction for the accountant in a selling role.

This concludes our brief overview of the marketing and selling world. Chapter 2 looks more closely at how the selling role affects you and how your attitude will contribute to the success you achieve.

Chapter Two

Your Role in Selling

Selling financial services is a new responsibility for many of you. To succeed you will need to learn different skills, hone ones that you already have, develop certain personal qualities, and most important, maintain a positive attitude toward this emerging role. Also, you are not going to sell full-time. Until selling becomes a more specialized function in the accounting profession, you will need to work it into your present job along with all your other duties.

YOUR CURRENT RESPONSIBILITIES

To get an idea of the scope of your current job, let's look at some of the major responsibilities you now have. You could be one or more of the following: an auditor who gives an opinion about a company's financial position and operating results, an organizer of financial information who reduces a mass of detail to comprehensible proportions, a tax adviser who helps businesses and individuals prepare returns and recommends tax economies, or a management adviser who helps businesses improve their efficiency and make maximum use of their resources.

Incorporated in any of these responsibilities are challenging demands, one of which is the sheer quantity of knowledge required for you to keep up and understand business and economic issues as well as complicated accounting and tax matters. Also, technical and reporting issues have increased in both frequency and complexity, demanding more time to maintain and improve technical and professional skills. An example is the increase in accounting series releases (ASRs) over the years. The Securities and Exchange Commission produced an average of eighteen ASRs per year from 1972 to 1976 versus four per year during all the previous years of its history.

Your professional role also requires you to solve problems, use good judgment, and maintain satisfying relationships with your clients. All together, that's a pretty challenging set of demands; but that's not all. While your professional role provides your firm's income and takes up much of your time, you have a few additional duties. You may recruit students, act as an instructor, supervise and counsel subordinates, write research articles, give speeches, join professional societies, become involved in specialized industries, and support community projects. It is doubtful that you knew everything that was involved when you decided to become an accountant. One CPA describes his varied responsibilities this way:

I thought when I entered public accounting that I would be spending almost all my time with clients, using my technical skills. That was true until right after I made senior. Then I realized that my continued success would depend more upon my people skills than upon my technical skills. And when I became manager I was expected to expand my skills and interests to include still more varied types of work. And since becoming partner, my time reports reflect an incredible variety of business activities. I'm still involved in the technical parts of the job, but frankly I consider myself to be more of an executive than an accountant.

ADDING THE SELLING ROLE

Making time for all these activities is an obvious problem. Priorities must be determined, deadlines met, and time wasters avoided. Even though internal and external pressures have increased, you still must maintain quality standards and achieve profit goals. These business and client demands may at times conflict with personal and family obligations. Now, marketing and selling are added to your present weight of responsibilities.

How heavy is this added weight? Can it be effectively carried along with everything else? Maybe. In a later chapter, we will take a closer look at how you arrange your time and what you may need to change to make room for the new selling role.

Clearly one factor in your chance for success will be how you feel about selling. Do you view it as just another task to do when you get around to it, or do you feel the way some accountants quoted here do?

I feel very strongly about the need for me to sell. We don't have a separate sales force. If I don't do it, who will? It would be nice to be able to sit back and let others do it, but that wouldn't happen. The environment has really changed in the last few years. I mean, competition has gotten so much stronger. I know a lot of partners in the other firms in this city and they're hustling. I'll be damned if I'm going to let them take business away from us.

Obviously, I take selling very seriously or I would not have the results I've gotten. As a matter of fact, I tell the whole office how important it is. Otherwise, everyone is going to think that someone else is going to take care of it. I used to see selling as something I could do pretty much by myself, but now that I run the office I've got to get others involved.

Clearly, some CPAs take the selling responsibility very seriously, and as the competition continues to get hotter we can expect to see more of them involved. Yet, there are a large number of accountants who grudgingly give lip service to selling and actually stay as far away as possible from getting involved. Usually, they say that they don't have the time, but their more successful peers suggest that there may be other reasons:

I suspect that they are afraid to try. It can be kind of scary to ask someone for their business and run the risk of getting turned down.

Selling isn't like accounting. Accounting and auditing can be tough at times, but most of the time it adds up. You're sure of your answer or you can look it up. There are no sure answers in selling; every situation is different and some people just don't like that uncertainty.

*Some of these guys have been around for a while. They probably re-
member when it was less competitive . . . when we got our business
because of our reputation for doing quality work, or from referrals.
They can't conceive of having to get out and beat the bushes.*

*They don't know how to sell. That's OK. None of us had sales courses
in college. But they don't even want to learn, and selling has to be
learned, just like any other skill.*

Many of the reasons for poor selling or for not even trying apparently are based on fear or a negative attitude toward the selling role.
This contrasts sharply with the positive attitude of those who succeed
at selling. In fact, those who succeed at selling see it not only as their
responsibility but as the preferred part of their job, as suggested by
these comments:

*Sure I enjoy it. Why? It's win/lose. I like to win, and in selling you
win or you lose. You get the client or you don't. There is no question
about how good a job you did. The results are very clear.*

*No question about it. I would rather sell than do anything else. Sell-
ing gives you a chance to help someone solve their problems, and problem solving is what I really enjoy doing.*

*I get a big jolt out of bringing in a new client. It's a high. I would
rather be out selling than doing anything else. Frankly, being responsible for running a department, with all that administrative crap, is a
pain.*

So we see that the CPA/consultant who is a successful salesperson
enjoys the role and prefers it to many other parts of the job. However,
enjoying the role is not sufficient. A number of skills and other requirements must be mastered if you are to succeed. One of these is
the need to know and understand absolutely and exactly what you
are trying to sell.

UNDERSTANDING YOUR SERVICES

Understanding your services is so obvious a requirement for selling
them that one would think it unnecessary to mention. Yet, every
year, an incredible number of sales are lost because the salesperson
did not know enough about his or her product or service to satisfy the

prospect's questions. As a result, the prospect lost confidence in the salesperson and the meeting ended with no sale.

We could, from time to time, expect that you might not know as much as you would like about your prospect's business, but there is never an excuse for not knowing about and understanding the services of your own firm. Here is testimony to the kind of regrettable experience that can occur:

I've always felt pretty comfortable talking about my firm's services to clients and prospective clients. I thought I knew all I had to know, until one day at a Rotary Club meeting someone asked me about a new software program that he heard our firm had just developed. He began asking some questions about the product that were not that technical, but I could not provide the answers. In fact, he knew more about my product than I did. I was really embarrassed, and I think I lost some credibility with him.

We are not suggesting that you must have an intimate knowledge of every service your firm provides, but you should have at least a basic understanding of what all your services can do for a client, and you should be able to explain that understanding. Let's list a few reasons why it's so important for you to be able to do this.

1. You will walk into a sales meeting with a lot more confidence.
2. You will be better able to answer some of the tough questions and objections that a prospect is apt to raise.
3. You will be able, should the need arise, to effectively shift your discussion from one service to another.
4. You will be better able to counter some of the selling points of your competition.
5. You won't overtalk in discussing your services; your comments will be brief, crisp, and to the point.
6. You will gain respect from the prospect who will be impressed with your knowledge and your ability to express that knowledge.

These are just a few reasons why you need to fully understand your own specialized service and have a working knowledge of your firm's other services. How do you manage to acquire what appears to be an overwhelming amount of information? Before we give a few sources, let's be realistic. You cannot afford to spend an excessive amount of time acquiring these data; you have many other responsibilities. The idea is to spend your time productively.

First, determine the information that you absolutely *must* know—the key issues and principles. Learn them fully so that you can explain them to others in whatever detail is required. Second, determine what you *should* know, the information that is important, but not as important as what you *must* know. Understand this information so that you can discuss the major issues with credibility. If necessary, you can delve deeper into this material to increase your knowledge. Finally, determine the information you *could* know, the information that is nice to know but which may not be worth the time or trouble to acquire. The must-know, should-know, and could-know information will vary, depending on what your specific function is, so be prepared to change your priorities as required.

Now, where do you get this information? The most obvious source is the knowledge you pick up each day in the course of doing your job, the problems you work on, the people you speak to, and the literature that crosses your desk. However, that is not really enough if you are to master your subject and have others perceive you as an expert. You have got to dig further, and here are some sources:

1. Start with your own office library, reviewing any publications or papers that have been written. If your office does not have a library, then check out the business departments of public libraries. They may not have extensive material, but at the very least they can direct you to other sources.
2. Call your local or state society or the American Institute of Certified Public Accountants (AICPA) for their latest publications on the subject you are studying.
3. Discuss the most current issues in your field with associates in your office or other offices.
4. Talk to your competition. If you can submerge your ego and do most of the questioning and listening, you can pick up good information.
5. Read the trade journals and magazines that cover your areas of interest and expertise. Industry associations regularly publish articles on pertinent issues and problems. Prospects of yours in a particular industry probably read them, and this will give you something to discuss with them.
6. Attend seminars that offer programs in your field. The quality of these seminars will vary, but with a little research you should be able to determine whether a particular seminar is right for you. It's a good idea to call before you sign up to find out who the speakers are and how they plan to conduct the seminar. In general, all-day lectures are less productive than seminars that plan for group discussions and other types of audience participation. Don't expect that every or, for that matter, any seminar will be a total winner.

Few are, and if you pick up a few good ideas and a deeper under-standing of the subject, you can consider it a worthwhile experience.

7. Get interested in a service or function in which you normally do not work. If you are primarily an auditor and a new tax ruling comes out, don't merely discuss it with a tax associate; ask to get involved in an actual problem your associate is working on—not a highly complex one, but one that will allow you to see all the elements of the ruling that affect the particular problem. You can do the same for that person in your field of knowledge.

Of course, acquiring knowledge and information is one job; re-membering it is another. Most of us are not blessed with photo-graphic memories. You need to develop a method for organizing your information so that you can recall it when needed. A simple filing system may work well, or you may want to consider a microcomputer that is capable of handling large amounts of information that can be easily accessed and updated.

This has been an overview of understanding your services. It's a short message, but an important one. You must have a thorough knowledge of your own business before you try to understand the prospect's business.

Understanding your own business is just one of several things you need to know and do to sell your services successfully. The following chapters will examine a number of other required skills. You will see that these skills fall into a very logical sequence as you go through the selling process. Knowing this sequence can be helpful, as evidenced by the following quote:

I've been selling our services for several years, and I guess I thought
the sale just happened at some point; you know, a little luck and a
little personal chemistry. Now, I understand that there is a progres-
sive thinking and communication process that takes place. It's like a
map that guides you from your first step to your final destination with
several stops along the way. That's the way I now look at a sale, and
most important, I can tell what point I'm at in any sale and that gives
me direction and a tremendous feeling of confidence.

Before looking at the first step in the selling process, however, you need to understand why prospects would want to buy your services, the subject of Chapter 3.

Chapter Three

Why Prospects Buy

First, you must understand and accept that a sale is based on a buying decision. Salespeople do not really sell anything, whether product or service. Rather they help to create a condition in the prospect's mind that is favorable to buying. This favorable condition is influenced by several factors that will be covered in the ensuing chapters. The chief factor in buying is the prospect's realization that his expectations, needs, and deepest motivations are being fulfilled by the product or service. Therefore, it is important for you, the salesperson, to identify, understand, and satisfy his requirements.

Recognize that people are different and that, consequently, their expectations, needs, and motivations are often different, even sometimes as they relate to the same product or service. Thus two of your prospects may look at your audit, tax, or other services with completely different perceptions even though the services are substantially the same. This will greatly influence the way you pursue each of these selling opportunities. This chapter examines some of the expectations, needs, and motivations of your prospects as they relate to buying your services.

THE PROSPECT'S BUSINESS EXPECTATIONS

Let's first examine what prospects expect from their accounting firm, whether we are talking about audits, tax advice, or management services. Although the following list is representative, you can probably add a few of your own requirements. Obviously, there is no ranking to these items, since any one could be of primary importance to a particular prospect.

- Professional competence
- Industry expertise
- Knowledge of the client's organization
- Ability to anticipate problems
- Ability to solve problems
- General business counsel
- Sounding board to test ideas
- New ideas and innovative approaches
- Guidance for future directions
- Bottom-line awareness
- Responsiveness to client needs and requests
- Completion of work on time
- Consistent effort and service
- Good human relations
- Value for the fee

Following are brief explanations of each of these business expectations.

Professional Competence. Prospects expect you to be knowledgeable about your own work. Competence is a given. They want professionals who are current with the latest laws and regulations and who can apply that knowledge to their organizations. Often there is no other source for them to turn to for answers to their questions. Some may feel that this is an obvious requirement, but you know people in your field who really don't have this high standard for knowledge or who once did but who are now hopelessly obsolete in their skills because they did not keep up.

Industry Expertise.   There is a constant need to develop an expertise in a particular industry. Over the last several years, as in any period in history, some industries have decreased in number and importance or even died out. Others, for example, health care and high-tech industries, have become prominent. Prospects assume that their accountants will understand the special language and problems of their particular industry. They don't want to hold clinics to teach their accountants the fine points of that industry. Industry expertise becomes even more important with larger clients because of the greater breadth and depth of the situations encountered.

Knowledge of the Client's Organization.   The demanding prospect or client expects his accountants at some point to become really interested in and familiar with his organization in addition to being knowledgeable about the industry as a whole. Thus the accountant must make an effort to get involved in areas of the client's business that are not required for the accounting work but that do represent opportunities for making a greater contribution. Of course, the prospect cannot absolutely expect this before hiring, so it is important that the accountant create this impression during the selling opportunity.

Ability to Anticipate Problems. Many accountants visualize themselves as problem solvers, and some truly have that talent. Prospects certainly appreciate this skill, but just as important, they like their accountants to anticipate problems so as to avoid them. This takes a more intuitive skill that is not the talent of everyone. However, those accountants who have this ability should use their research to come up with ways of demonstrating their ability during the selling meeting by referring to possible problems the prospect may be facing in the near future.

Ability to Solve Problems.   Even if the accountant is good at anticipating and avoiding problems, there are still going to be problems. Prospects expect the accountant to identify accurately the real problem, pinpoint some of the causes, and recommend practical solutions that have a good chance of working. During the selling process, the accountant should be able to provide evidence of this problem-solving ability. A later chapter discusses how to communicate this skill.

General Business Counsel. Many prospects will want their accountants to provide counsel for more general business problems. This is a reasonable expectation considering the variety of experiences that most accountants have in dealing with the wide range of client businesses.

Sounding Board to Test Ideas. Some prospects will look to their accountants to be sounding boards for testing ideas and offering objective opinions as to their feasibility. This is a valuable function for the accountant because the prospect may not have anyone in his organization that can play that role. The last thing a chief executive officer (CEO) needs is another "yes man."

New Ideas and Innovative Approaches. In addition to acting as sounding boards for their clients, accountants have the chance to offer new ideas and suggestions of their own. Normally this is done in the financial and control areas in the course of the audit and is communicated in a management letter. The accountant comes in contact with many other areas of the business; she has the opportunity to suggest ideas and make recommendations for increased efficiency and better operating results in these areas. To suggest that this would be a conflict of interest or outside the responsibility of the CPA is absurd and an excuse not to get involved in a process of innovative thought.

Guidance for Future Directions. Traditionally, accountants have been viewed by many clients as being most comfortable working with the past and present, that is, reviewing the last year's operations and giving an opinion that the numbers as of a certain date are fairly presented and reasonably reflect the company's current financial condition. Certainly, historical information is of some value to the client, but the accountant can be of far greater value if she can relate these data to the client's future plans. The client may not expect this help, but he would certainly appreciate receiving it and would view the accountant with greater respect as a result.

Bottom-Line Awareness. With the exception of not-for-profit organizations, the name of the game in business is to make a profit, and profits come from increased revenue and decreased costs. If an accountant is to grow beyond her traditional image and become more of a businessperson for her client, she needs to acquire the knack of translating her observations into consequences that affect both the top and bottom lines.

Responsiveness to Client Needs and Requests.   Prospective clients expect their accountants to be responsive and to provide answers to their questions in time to make the right decisions. Being unresponsive to client needs is one of the biggest complaints that clients have about their accountants, and for the most part this complaint is justified. Prospects look wth skepticism at CPAs who promise during the selling meeting that they will be responsive. Some type of evidence must be provided by the accountants to give greater credence to their promised responsiveness.

Completion of Work.   Equally important to prospective clients is the assurance that their work will be completed on time. This can be a particularly sensitive point for a prospect from a smaller organization who may fear that larger clients will come first. Obviously this can be a tough problem when all clients want their work completed on time within a time frame that is compressed into a few months of the year, but some CPA firms have minimized this problem with innovative scheduling that moves parts of the audit to other times of the year.

Consistent Effort and Service.   The prospect wants consistently good service and expects that the accounting firm will not start off with a big flourish and then gradually decrease the effort. Imagine the letdown when the senior on the job is replaced every couple of years without an effort by the partner or manager to compensate for the interrupted service.

Good Human Relations.   Clients expect accountants assigned to their engagements to fit into their environment and not to disrupt or cause animosity with their employees. Unfortunately, some accountants use poor human relations on the job. They project an air of superiority and are otherwise rude and demanding, particularly to lower-level employees. There is never an excuse for this or similar behavior, and the prospect who senses this when interviewing a prospective accounting firm would be wise to keep looking.

Value for the Fee.   Prospective clients expect and deserve value for their money. This is not a discussion about what is the right fee—that is an entirely different matter. We are talking about the potential problem of a client feeling that he is being taken advantage of. Sometimes clients feel this way when they are asked to pay increasingly higher fees and do not see additional value. The prospect should always feel that he is getting his money's worth and maybe a little more.

Those are some of the expectations that prospective clients have. You probably cannot meet all expectations for all of your clients, but don't get discouraged. Most clients will accept less than what they want in *some* of their expectations provided that they have their *most important* expectation(s) fulfilled. It's up to you to find out which are the really important expectations for each prospective client.

THE PROSPECT'S PERSONAL EXPECTATIONS

We have just looked at a pretty extensive list of prospects' business expectations. Now let's look at some of the less tangible personal expectations they may have.

Rapport.   Prospects want to be comfortable with their accountants. Call it chemistry, rapport, or whatever, it's the prospect's feeling that says, "We can work together." This does not necessarily entail a very close personal relationship, but you do need to have mutual respect.

Trust.   Even more important to the prospect is her expectation that she can completely trust her accountants. Obviously, respecting confidential matters is a professional requirement that is assumed. Trust involves the consideration that the accountant is involved in decisions that could greatly affect the financial health of the prospect's organization. The prospect must believe that she is getting the best possible advice.

Empathy.   Prospects expect their accountants to have empathy—to be able to see things from the other person's point of view. This does not mean that you feel the way your client feels, but it does mean that you understand the way he feels, particularly when he is experiencing a difficult situation. If you have thoroughly done your research before you meet with the prospect, you will have an excellent opportunity to demonstrate your empathy when you do have your meeting.

Personal Attention. You might call it ego, or the desire to feel important, but many prospects expect that they are going to get the personal attention of the partner on the job. They want the partner to be available to them. This requirement may be so strong that they are willing to put up with other shortcomings. Also, sometimes a prospect will expect to talk to her accountant about more personal subjects and get his opinion, for example, about family problems or personal investments. The accountant needs to handle this one carefully so that he provides the support that the prospect or client expects but does not make the decisions.

Socializing. In certain situations the prospect expects to have a more personal relationship with his accountant, such as a golf or tennis companion or someone to join the Friday night poker game. This can be a very advantageous situation provided it fits your idea of a good time.

THE PROSPECT'S MOTIVATIONAL NEEDS

On a broader scale, the prospect's business and personal expectations are often the result of much deeper motivational needs, needs that directly affect people and the choices they make in an effort to lead happy, productive lives. Lists of motivational needs have been made by a wide range of authorities. Although it is impossible to completely describe each of these needs, it is important for salespeople to understand how individual motivations influence buying decisions. The following are some generally recognized motivators:

- Survival
- Security
- Belonging
- Recognition

- Comfort
- Achievement
- Power
- Love and affection
- Creativity
- Adventure
- Health
- Money

Whenever possible, relate them to your selling situation. As you read them, keep a couple of things in mind. Although everyone shares all these motivations to a certain extent, each person will have one or two that will be of primary importance. In other words, people are different. The primary needs are fairly consistent over a person's life but can shift to reflect individual growth or a significant change in that person's life. Also, the fulfillment of these needs is often the driving force behind a person's decisions, including buying decisions. Finally, remember that anything you can do to help someone satisfy his or her needs will make you valuable in that person's life. The following discusses each motivator individually.

Survival. Survival is the lowest need level and describes a person's need for food, drink, shelter, clothing, and sex. In today's society, with the exception of certain developing countries, these needs are pretty much satisfied, although maybe not always to the extent that some would like. But, for the most part, survival in the sense used here is not a critical issue.

However, survival in the business world is another story. An entrepreneur who has staked every penny she has on a new, risky business venture may be very close to bankruptcy, or a senior executive whose operation is suffering critical losses may be on the brink of being fired. Both these people are tottering on the edge of economic survival, and you may be in a position to help them.

Security. The next motivator is not quite as crucial as survival, although it may seem to be to those who have it as a primary motivational need. Generally, these people are very concerned with holding on to what they possess, whether it be tangible goods or a particular position in life. Their personal assets as you might expect will mainly consist of cash, government bonds, and other safe investments. Don't be surprised if their homes have a healthy supply of window bars, locks, and alarms.

In the business environment you could expect them to favor a conservative approach, one that will emphasize the protection of assets rather than the "big kill." They will shy away from risk, and if you suggest anything new, they will want almost complete assurance that it will work. As people draw closer to retirement, security may play a larger part in their business decisions, and they may follow the well-known philosophy of "don't blow it, you've only got a couple of years to go." As you might expect, these people often bring the state of worry to an art. Take advantage of this emotional state by giving them assurance and peace of mind.

Belonging. This is an interesting motivational need because it can be expressed in so many ways. It involves being part of a larger group of people and sharing practices, experiences, and culture. It binds ethnic groups together, forces teenagers to dress the same, and forms the essence of national pride and patriotism. This is not the need of the loner or the individualist; it is the need of someone who wants to belong to a group. In business, as in their personal lives, these people will often look to emulate people they respect or admire, perhaps because they are not sure of their own judgment. Consequently, their decision to buy may be based on what their role models have bought.

Recognition. We all know people who have a strong need for recognition. It is satisfied in a number of ways. Some look to acquire material goods that are a visible sign of their success or chosen lifestyle. Some thrive on titles or other marks of special status. Still others want to see their names mentioned in public. However they choose to express it, these people all share one characteristic, the need to feel important in their own eyes and in the eyes of others. Acknowledgment by others is particularly satisfying to them.

In business these people can be identified by the size of their offices, the costly furniture, the well-known pieces of art, and the other trappings that separately mean little but collectively draw a picture of someone crying out for attention. In a selling situation, these people can be favorably influenced if they perceive that the results of your services will help them gain recognition and a sense of importance in their organization. Unlike those who have a need for security, these prospects like to make up their own minds in deciding whether to buy, or at least they like to think they are doing this. Therefore, when selling to them, do not come on too strong, but rather suggest ideas and let them think the ideas are theirs.

Comfort.   Most of us share the need for comfort. It is perfectly natural to want to enjoy the comforts of life, good food, a pleasant lifestyle, interesting vacations, and a relaxing time by oneself or with companions. We have all experienced the need to forget everything and just take it easy for a while. However, for some people this desire becomes a very strong priority in their life, and many of their decisions are based on fulfilling this need. In the past few years, a number of young graduates have espoused the personal philosophy that there's more to life than work, and they pursue a lifestyle that supports this belief. Some will change their philosophy as they mature and develop other interests, but others will remain pretty well set in this primary need for comfort.

You will encounter these people in business, and some will be your prospects. You may recognize them by a "9-to-5" work habit, or a good part of their conversation may revolve around the comfort subject. They are not necessarily disinterested in their business role, but they are certainly not going to be the hard drivers who customarily put in 60 to 70 hours a week at the job. If you encounter them in a selling situation, try to present your services in a way that directly or indirectly contributes to their need for comfort.

Achievement.   Some people have a strong need to achieve, to see a visible accomplishment that tells them they are special. They are really not competing with others, although often their achievements will clearly outshine others. They are looking not for recognition from their peers or friends but rather for an affirmation of their own success. They will strive with unflagging commitment and energy to reach their objective, and they regard obstacles as challenges. Many breakthroughs in science and medicine have been accomplished by people with a strong need to achieve. Superstars in professional sports are also driven by a sense of excellence in their pursuit of outstanding and record-breaking performances.

People with a strong need to achieve often make it to the top in business and are responsible for major decisions. Because achievers respect other achievers, it is helpful if you are one. However, this is an added attraction, not a strict requirement for success in selling to these prospects. Probably your best bet is to identify with the truly outstanding goals and objectives that these people see for their companies and themselves. Don't talk about the mundane and routine aspects of your service; instead, show your appreciation of what they are trying to accomplish, and demonstrate how you can contribute to these goals.

Power.   Power brings out mixed feelings in people. We would all like to have more power than we have, but few of us are capable of acquiring it or doing what is necessary to achieve it. Those that have power are viewed with admiration, envy, distrust, hate, and a few other human emotions, not only because people with power can make significant things happen but also because their actions usually affect the lives of others, often without the others' consent. The most obvious seats of power lie in positions of authority: political officeholders who pass and administer laws, the police and other agencies who enforce the law, the military with the means to defend and kill, and even educators, who often have power over the direction of our future careers. This is not to say that all people in these positions choose to use this power, but those that do have a strong need to control their environment and the lives of those within that environment.

In business, power seekers will often gravitate to large organizations where there are more opportunities for them to exercise power. For example, some who head large conglomerates may have no great interest in any of the businesses they own or control, these businesses being only segments of a larger picture, to be bought, sold, or otherwise manipulated. And, of course, the larger the organization, the greater the control over people. It does not take a genius to see that the power seekers will look favorably on any consultant who can further their needs.

Love and Affection.   This is a motivation that most people need to express. There is a strong need to demonstrate love, affection, and caring for our families and others who are close to us. The success of many industries is based on this need, the most obvious being those that manufacture or sell personal items, which range all the way from a bouquet of flowers to a $100,000 piece of jewelry. A walk through any store at Christmas will attest to this need, although there are some skeptics who claim other motivational needs such as guilt or envy are at work. Take a look at some of the magazine advertisements and television commercials and see how many are aimed right at the buyer who needs to express affection.

Some find it difficult to relate this need to the buyer of accounting services. True, it is less obvious than the tangible items we have mentioned, but consider successful executives who are looking ahead with some anxiety to sending two or three of their children to the better colleges. The need to provide over $50,000 per child is a very strong motivation to make money. If you can in some way show how your services will help the organization save or make money that results in greater income to these people, you may be able to take advantage of this need.

Creativity. Some people have a strong urge to create, to form something that has not existed before, and to create it in a way that puts their own individual brand upon it. This is most clearly seen, for example, in the work of artists, musicians, designers, and those who invent new products and systems. You may also observe this in sports, where a coach will spend hours devising new offensive strategies and defensive patterns. A good share of the toy and hobby industries is devoted to giving buyers the raw materials to create and build their own finished products.

Business has its share of creative people, but they may be a little more difficult to identify, especially if you restrict your contacts to financial people, who may not have a strong need to create. Instead, look to entrepreneurs who invented or developed their first product or service. Even if they have since become successful business people, the chances are that deep inside they still carry the strong urge to create. Listen to their new ideas, and point out how your services can help bring these ideas to fruition.

Adventure. Adventure as referred to here is the need to have a new experience, to satisfy one's curiosity, and to be willing to take a risk to achieve the adventure. The last ingredient is important, because it eliminates those who would like to have adventure in their lives but are not willing to pay the price for the experience. As you might expect, the urge for adventure is strongest in younger people who are looking forward to experiencing life. As they grow older, only those who are really motivated by this need will continue to seek it out. For example, observe how the success of some businesspeople has been largely brought about by their desire and willingness to search out and invest in new business ventures. How do you fit into the world of the adventurers? It is doubtful that they expect you to take on the role of promoter, yet, if you have the skill or resources, you can assist them in mergers and acquisitions. They may really look to you as the balance to their adventurous spirit. However, don't let your natural inclination toward being conservative discourage these people, because then you will not fulfill their need.

Health. People have always been interested in maintaining good physical and mental health, and periodically there is a ground swell of medical and nonmedical advisers urging us via books, tapes, television programs, and classes to eat differently, exercise more, think positively, and otherwise improve our physical and mental wellness. Most people agree that this makes sense, although their actions (for example, countinuing to smoke) do not always follow their thinking. For some people the desire to maintain good health is stronger than in others. This desire may be caused by a number of reasons, anxiety about a poor family health history, fear of death or incapacitation, avoidance of pain, concern about providing for loved ones, vanity about one's appearance, or some degree of hypochondria. In any case they will go to great ends to overcome these health fears, rational or otherwise.

The desire for good health is based on both negative fears and positive benefits. For example, younger prospects may view the need for good health in a more positive vein, exulting in the feeling of energy that permits them to play football, ski, and engage in other strenuous activities. Their purchases and spending habits will support that way of thinking. But as they get older and the body parts start needing more maintenance, they become more concerned. After a certain age, they have more years to look back on than ahead to, and they begin to think of ways to preserve or even increase the number of remaining years. They begin special diets, visit health clubs several times a week, and maybe buy a vacation home in a warm climate.

As a human being you can personally relate to these needs. As a salesperson you can take advantage of them. This is not to suggest that you put M.D. after CPA or start selling pills and condominiums, but you should closely examine the consequences of your services to their businesses and determine what benefit, if any, ultimately affects their desire for good health.

Money. This topic has been saved for last because there is some question about whether money by itself is a motivational need. Some say it is the strongest need, and many salespeople embrace this point of view. Others say that money by itself is merely paper and that it is how the money is spent that determines the real need. This position also has its supporters. Let's examine the argument more closely.

Businesspeople are interested in making money or saving money— to make a profit is obviously a strong reason for being in business. Certainly, the prospect will be interested in seeing how this can be done, so if your service can achieve this aim, by all means use it in your selling strategy.

Keep in mind, however, that most businesspeople are bombarded daily with similar claims from newspapers, television commercials, direct mail pieces, and scores of salespeople. You therefore may not really be offering anything unique, and it will be difficult to sell your services on just that basis. Instead, think about what prospects would do if, in fact, the money gain or saving could be achieved. Would they put it into the bank to collect interest, buy another company, test a new product, make a big contribution, draw it out for personal use? In short, if you can combine the issue of saving or gaining money with its consequences (as determined by the buyer's primary motivation) you will be building a powerful selling strategy that will be difficult to resist.

This quick rundown of some of the basic motivational needs is not all-inclusive; you may think of others that will give you insight into the deeper motivations behind buying decisions. As you consider these motivations and think of the people you know, business and personal, you may say, "People have all of these motivations." Yes, they do, but not to the same degree. To some people power would be a nice thing to have; to others it is an all-consuming drive. The real test is when the situation demands that a person make a choice between two or more strong motivational needs that conflict with each other. Invariably the stronger need will win out. So use your research and questioning (more about those later) to ferret out the strongest needs and plan your strategy around them.

This concludes our discussion on why prospects buy. We have discussed their expectations of you from both a business and personal perspective and have covered the deeper motivations behind their buying decisions. Without an appreciation and understanding of such things, you cannot expect to succeed in selling your services. Chapter 4 will use this information to start building your selling strategy.

SKILL-BUILDING TECHNIQUES

1. List your target prospects and the key person you will be selling to in each organization. Next to each name write what you consider to be their major business and personal expectations of you and your firm.
2. Using the same list, write what you consider to be the top two or three motivational needs that each person has and the reasons why you believe this to be so. In each question, if you do not know the answer, plan to find out in the near future.

Chapter Four

Making Contact

Selling professional services, as we discussed earlier, differs in several ways from selling products. One difference is that professionals generally do not solicit prospects, although there seems to be a trend toward exactly that. But, for the present, you probably meet most potential clients through an introduction, some type of meeting, or an informal occasion. Usually, your initial conversation is built around a common interest or small talk. Possibly, as you get to know each other, an opportunity arises for you to begin a business relationship.

Obviously you are not going to start knocking on the doors of strangers, but you still must find ways to make that first contact with prospective clients. Thus you must take the initiative just as a product salesperson would.

TAKING THE INITIATIVE

As a CPA you are accustomed to meeting prospective clients in a variety of business, social, and other types of occasions. You are also used to having some of these prospects eventually become clients. Often, this process depends on the propect's getting to know you and what your firm does and on his deciding that you could be of value to him. In short, the prospect is involved in a buying decision, and you hope to benefit by his decision.

What is probably less usual for you is to take control of this potential relationship at the start, to take the initiative in making that initial contact with the prospect. This is the first step in a potential sale. Unfortunately, some professionals see this as being overly aggressive, unethical, or unprofessional. Luckily, others take a different view:

Whenever I meet a new person, it's always in the back of my mind that this could be a potential client. Granted, most times nothing happens. But if there's a chance of it working out, I want to get it moving. I call that taking control of the sale.

Before proceeding, let us take a closer look at *initiative*, the first essential quality that must be understood and used if one is to be successful at selling or, for that matter, at accomplishing anything of importance anywhere. First, a dictionary definition: initiative means "taking the first step toward a desired action." A sales manager of a successful consulting firm describes a salesperson with initiative as "somebody who does things without being told to do them."

Here is how one CPA who is successful at selling his firm's services talks about the importance of initiative:

Certainly it's important to be the one who starts the ball rolling. Maybe someday our office and expertise will be so well known that I'll just sit here and watch the work roll in. But right now I go after it. It's funny when you talk about initiative. I've never really considered myself a pushy kind of guy, the hard-sell type. Yet, when I look back at some of the things I've achieved, it's because I've gone after them. Yes, taking the initiative is a must to bring in business.

Not all CPAs show initiative in the sales area. Some confuse taking the initiative with being too aggressive. Certainly, clients are often doubtful about their accountants' initiative, particularly when they are not getting active help in solving their business problems. Here is one CPA's comment on initiative as it relates to his peers:

*Important to take the initiative? Absolutely, but I will bet you could
ask every partner in this firm that question and you'd get the same
answer. Except that, for many of them, initiative in selling means en-
couraging bankers and clients to refer prospects to us. To me that's the
absolute minimum degree of initiative needed to bring in clients.*

Another expresses a feeling of frustration at the passiveness he sees
in his partners:

*We've got too many partners sitting around waiting for something to
happen. It's part of the "If you're good, people will hear about it and
come running to be your client" syndrome. That just doesn't work
anymore, at least I don't see many prospects breaking our door down.*

How about your own initiative? Take a close look at yourself, particularly your past experiences, and try to determine under what
circumstances you held back and watched things happen. Did this
happen primarily when you faced an unfamiliar situation? Was there
a high degree of risk or failure involved? Was there potential for
embarrassment?

Any one of these situations can immobilize most people in the
selling role. Why accept this inertia as a permanent disability? If you
are willing to accept the possibility of rejection, risk of failure, and
facing the unfamiliar as conditions of life, then you can proceed.

Examine this subject from a more positive view. Can you recall
times when you did take the initiative? Perhaps it was a leadership
position in school, a critical personal decision, or, more recently, a
sensitive client situation. Remember the results? I would guess that
you have good feelings about what happened. If you have taken the
initiative before, you can do it again. However, you must make a real
commitment, because successful selling requires a concentrated effort
and unflagging devotion to getting that client—making that sale.

OPPORTUNITIES FOR MAKING CONTACT

Having made the commitment to take the initiative, the next step is to
identify opportunities to meet prospects and generally to become
visible to those who may buy your service. Here are some options.

If you are well known in a special field, you may be asked to speak
to groups who share your interest in that subject. Take advantage of
these opportunities. It is an excellent way to demonstrate your exper-

tise to a large number of people at one time. One CPA who uses this technique successfully says:

I present papers on various tax subjects. To get on the program I need to get to know the program chairmen and suggest topics to them. I don't pick a subject that's 6 months old; it has to be of current interest. Before preparing the talk, I try to find out who is going to be in the audience so I can tailor my comments to specific people in the audience that I want to know better.

To succeed at giving presentations, you must keep up with current issues, be willing to put in the required time to prepare a carefully constructed talk, and develop your speaking skills so that you come across well to your audience.

Conducting seminars is somewhat similar to making a presentation. You need to know your subject, to aim it at certain members of the audience, and to have good speaking skills. However, there are differences. For example, if it is your responsibility to run the seminar, then you need to do the necessary marketing to get the audience to attend. You also have to plan how you intend to follow up sales leads after the seminar.

Another difference between a straight presentation and a seminar is in how it is conducted. Often, a presentation may be nothing more than a 25-minute dissemination of information, with little audience participation except for a question-and-answer period. At a seminar an audience expects to participate more, which may require you to plan discussion groups and other interactive devices. Also, you will probably need to get other members of your firm involved in presenting the material and conducting the program, so you will need to be sure that they have the necessary instructional and speaking skills.

Do not forget such administrative details as registration, lunch, adequate light and comfortable temperature in the room, functioning audiovisual equipment, and a hundred other details that can make or break your seminar. For these matters, it makes sense to know what you are doing or to assign someone to that role. Fortunately, there is a good deal of material available on how to run seminars. Your library or some of the local associations are excellent sources for this type of information.

Fostering relationships with the firm's alumni is another way to make contact with prospective clients. Schedule regular opportunities to meet with them, for example, a golf outing or group dinner. Assign a member of your firm to talk to each of them. If the alumni are already clients, look for ways to expand existing business. For those who are not clients, try to find out about their relationship with their present accountants or some problem with which they are wrestling. Although you do not want to appear too aggressive, do not be afraid to let them know you are interested in having them as clients.

Joining a professional association, community organization, or social club continues to be an option that many CPAs use to meet prospective clients. If you wish to do so, here are a few guidelines for maximizing the results.

First, join an organization whose activities you enjoy. Never join a group solely for the purpose of meeting prospects. If you do not really enjoy being involved in the organization, the chances are you will not become active and, consequently, will not get to know the other members very well. After a while, you will become bored and find reasons not to attend meetings. Consider the contrasting experiences of this CPA:

I was involved in the Rotary Club for 10 years but never got one lead. I guess I was waiting for them to come to me. Frankly, that whole experience was rather forgettable even though I was treasurer and director. On the other hand, a couple of years ago my son and I joined Indian Guides, a group of eight fathers and sons. I thought it would be a good way to spend time with my son. Three of those fathers are now tax clients, and I don't really remember pushing for the business, but I did get to know them and I was interested in helping them.

Ask yourself, "What are my interests? Sports? Art? Music? Working with children?" Do you have hobbies that you could share with others who have similar hobbies? Accountants provide such a variety of services today that it is difficult to imagine any group of people that could not benefit from at least one service you offer. If they have no need, they may have a friend, relative, or associate who could benefit. A word of caution: Do not expect that an organization composed entirely or mostly of other CPAs is going to provide much in the way of business. Be clear about the purpose of the organization and its membership before you make your choice.

If you do decide to join an organization, get elected or appointed to an office as soon as possible or, at the very least, volunteer for a committee. This will quickly get you interacting with others. A number of people join organizations and never do more than show up at the meetings. You can spot this type pretty easily. He is usually standing alone with a glass in his hand waiting for someone else to initiate an introduction, or he spends the whole night talking to people he knows and makes no effort to meet others. Approaching a stranger, even in a meeting of common interest, is difficult for most of us. Sometimes we feel we need a good reason to do it. As an officer of an organization with the responsibility for making others feel welcome, you have a built-in reason for walking up to people you have never met and opening up a conversation.

Invariably, when CPAs join organizations, they are asked to be the treasurer. That is a good start because it gets you involved quickly in a function in which you are knowledgeable and comfortable. However, the treasurer's office does not provide the same kind of leadership or visibility you could get if you were president or if you chaired an important committee. Here is advice from one CPA:

I'm quite active when I get involved; I'm a big advocate of getting to be chairman of the membership committee. When I held this office with my local alumni association, we brought in 142 members, which was an all-time record. From that activity I got to know many of these people quite well and subsequently picked up several new clients. Several others indicated to me that as soon as they moved into a little stronger position in their company they would try to work us in as their accountants.

To review, if you enjoy organization work, select one with an activity in which you have an interest, become active in that organization, and aim to hold an office that gives you leadership and visibility.

You may even be able to acquire a client through a chance meeting while traveling. For example, some accountants systematically travel first class for the specific purpose of creating an opportunity to meet high-level executives, consciously creating a good opportunity to have a top executive as a captive audience for 2 or 3 hours. More often than not, it will be just pleasant conversation, but every once in a while you can make a good connection that can be followed up later. The obvious point is to take advantage of every opportunity, opening your horizons to what is possible.

Sometimes taking advantage of the situation means keeping your eyes and ears open to opportunities. A colleague relates an example of this technique:

Not long after I became partner in charge of this office, we had a new mayor elected. I knew he had to make a decision whether he wanted to keep the city's present auditors. I called one of our clients and asked him to introduce me to the mayor. Through connections I was able to get the interview, and this led to our getting the engagement. Looking back, my success was first due to taking advantage of an opportunity

that others may not have seen. Second, I was able to use the influence
of people I knew to get this interview. I believe it's important to know
as many people in your city as possible. It's hard work but those are
the contacts that eventually pay off for you.

Just keeping your eyes and ears open is not all it takes to meet a prospective client. Plan that initial contact so that you can make the best use of your time as well as meet the right people.

PLANNING THE INITIAL CONTACT

People who "think" sales generally have a very clear plan of action when they enter a room of potential customers. They have found out ahead of time who will be at the meeting and have decided which ones are viable clients. If you select this strategy, plan your time to reach as many of your targeted people as possible. This requires that you gracefully introduce yourself into conversations and just as gracefully make an exit to move on to another prospect. One way to disengage yourself from a conversation is to introduce the person you are talking with to another person.

If the situation is a dinner, obviously having your prime target prospect seated next to you is desirable. A way to accomplish this is to make your prime prospect the last person you talk to before the call to dinner. If there is no set seating, it is relatively easy to suggest that the two of you find a table.

If you have not selected target prospects to meet that evening, try then to meet as many new people as possible. Most organization meetings provide name tags for members and guests, and often the person's company or business is also identified. Whether or not name tags are provided, quickly commit the person's name to memory. If you have difficulty remembering names, take a course or read one of the books that teach you how to do this. In a world where people have trouble remembering other people's names, you can stand apart as someone who cares enough to make the effort.

Obviously, you want to present a friendly, cheerful image to those you meet. If you had a really lousy day and are worried or depressed, you may not want to attend the meeting unless you can put your troubles temporarily out of the way and get into the spirit of the evening. Remember, nobody is really interested in your problems. They've got enough of their own.

FROM SOCIAL TALK TO BUSINESS OPPORTUNITY

The initial contact with a prospect often takes the form of a social, impersonal conversation, a way of getting acquainted in a relatively relaxed and nonthreatening situation. Nevertheless, if an initial conversation is to turn into a business discussion, you must be able to move gracefully from small talk to more substantive issues. One CPA does it this way:

I keep an information file on what is happening in various industries, articles from trade journals and business magazines like Forbes *and* Fortune. *Before I attend a meeting, I try to find out who is going to be there and what industry they're in. I'll pick one or two target prospects and review the most current information I have on file, or I'll call someone who knows something about that industry. That evening I'll make sure I have some conversation with my target and, at the appropriate time, I'll comment or ask a question on that information. It's a little work up front, but it really helps zero in on meaningful business information.*

Sometimes though, you will not have time to prepare in advance. Then other methods can be used to develop information. Most people like to talk about themselves and the question, "How did you happen to get into the business you are in?" is one that invariably gets them talking. From there, it is easy to probe for other business subjects. If you are used to observing the behavior of others, you may be able to detect a worried or distracted expression on an individual's face. A comment like, "Your body's here but your mind must be back at the office. Is the problem that serious?" will usually evoke from that person a wry smile which may be followed by a disclosure of the problem. Some CPAs are talented at fitting their comments to the particular style of the prospect. The following is a contribution from one such CPA:

It depends on the kind of person I'm dealing with and how well I know him. If he's kind of reserved, I don't push too hard. On the other hand, if I know the other person is pretty open, I'll come right out and ask him about some aspect of his business. Sometimes I'm a little blunt. A few weeks ago at a party I saw a guy who I knew was having problems with his business, and when I got him alone, I said, "When the hell are you going to clear up that inventory situation?" He laughed and said he was still working on it. We talked a little more about it. He'll be a client someday.

You can move from social to business conversations by mentioning problems of other unidentified clients whose businesses are similar to that of the prospect. If you are traveling in a plane or train, you can place some current literature within sight, picking a subject that would be of interest to a broad group of business people, such as tax shelters. Once the prospect is talking about her business, stop talking and listen. Effective listening is a skill that everyone agrees is important, yet few people are really good at it. Being a good listener is more than just keeping quiet. It means listening actively, punctuating your silence with nods and occasional questions or comments. It means tuning out other distractions and keeping your eyes from wandering away from the prospect.

DEMONSTRATING YOUR INTEREST AND EXPERTISE

Sometimes a prospect is wrestling with a business problem but may be reluctant to share it with you because he is embarrassed or feels he does not know you well enough. He may disguise the problem by expressing it in another way. It is up to you to get at the real problem. Here's how one CPA did this when he was seated next to a controller at a dinner:

During the course of the dinner he mentioned that he had been working late at night for several weeks and hadn't seen very much of his family. I showed concern for his situation and carefully probed for the reason why he was working so late. He told me that he had just installed a new computer system and was having all kinds of control problems. After asking a few more questions, I offered him a few ideas on how to attack his problem. We got into a deep discussion and at the end of the evening I offered to meet him at his office to explore the problem further. He took me up on the offer and today he's a client. If I hadn't picked up on his initial personal problem, I never would have surfaced the business problem.

So it is important to listen carefully for the effects of a problem; they can lead to the uncovering of the problem itself. Once you have identified the problem, demonstrate your expertise by offering a few ideas or suggestions, without attempting to solve the whole problem. The objective is to demonstrate a lot of your interest and a lesser amount of your knowledge. If you give the prospect just enough information to intrigue, you have an excellent chance to continue the discussion at a later date. If he does not invite you to his office, suggest a meeting yourself. You have a "live" prospect who may just be a little shy. If he does not take you up on your offer, don't push him. In the next day or two, send him some literature that will help with the problem; then follow up with a phone call.

In summary, a number of techniques can turn a social conversation into a business opportunity. The key points are to listen carefully, particularly for personal concern which may indicate business problems, to show interest and empathy, to probe tactfully, to demonstrate your expertise (not all of it), and to initiate another meeting.

Before discussing how to prepare for the next meeting, let's look at another way to contact prospective clients, one that takes a good deal of initiative and skill—use of the telephone.

TELEPHONE SELLING

Telephone selling has unique characteristics and whole books are devoted to the subject, but for our purposes, we need discuss only the principles and techniques that apply to selling services.

Some CPAs get a little nervous when they think about making a telephone call to a prospective client with the purpose of trying to make a sale. All the old "professional ethics" ghosts come tumbling out of the closet again. One CPA commented:

I really had a problem picking up the phone to make an unsolicited call. I thought the prospect was going to think I was pushy and unprofessional, and therefore think less of me. I guess I was too concerned about me. If I really had the prospect's interests in mind, I would have realized that he or she would want to speak to me if I had something of value for them.

Other real or imagined obstacles block our use of the telephone to approach the prospect. Among these are the problem of getting to the right person, the fear of talking to an unseen and sometimes unknown face, the inability to get a visual reaction to our remarks, and the concern about taking up the prospect's valuable time. These are all valid concerns, but all are surmountable.

The first and most important principle in telephone selling is to have a legitimate reason for your call. This is no different from the selling of a product or service or, for that matter, any other type of business call. Nobody appreciates being called just to pass the time.

Try to narrow your purpose for the call down to one or, at the most, two reasons. That is about all you can expect to handle in the available time.

Three types of calls come under the scope of telephone selling: the personal call, the follow-up call, and the cold call. The personal call is not for an immediate sale but rather tries to create an environment for potential future business. One CPA learned to do this after he himself had been a recipient of this practice:

We had just moved into this city about a month before when I received a call from one of the senior vice presidents of a local bank inviting my wife and me to a cocktail party welcoming new businesspeople to the city. At first I was a little curious about the invitation, but we wound up going and had a great time meeting new people and learning about things one wants to know when one moves to a new location. Soon after, he called me to discuss any mutual business interests we might have. I have since incorporated this idea into my own activities. I don't hold big cocktail parties for everyone, but I do contact new businesspeople in town whom I think I might like to know better. I'll invite them to a community activity where they can meet others. One of these people has since become a client.

The personal call is a relatively low-key effort that can produce positive results. Your spouse might also see an opportunity to contact and welcome another person's spouse. This would be a good way to have your spouse get involved in your marketing activity.

As mentioned earlier, following up with a call to a prospect you have met earlier offers an excellent way to pursue a selling opportunity. If you impressed the prospect with your interest and ability, then you can expect to have the person welcome your call. Even if your initial meeting was less than spectacular, you still have a good chance to get the prospect's ear. Let's go through the strategies for making the most of the phone call.

First, know exactly why you are making the call and what you hope to accomplish. With few exceptions, it is not the purpose of the call to make a sale. It is virtually impossible to sell professional services on the phone. Your purpose is to arrange for a meeting. Again, narrow your purpose down to one or two points. That's all you can explain and about as much as the prospect can concentrate on in the brief time you have.

Collect all the available data about the subject. Review in your mind the conversation you had with the prospect and determine what his particular interest was. Study it carefully so you feel confident that you can answer most any question that may arise. Select one piece of information that you believe will capture his attention, something he will want to hear more about. This could be startling information, a provocative question, an immediate benefit, a potential answer to a problem, an explanation of how something works. In most cases, it should deal with some aspect of the prospect's business. Think of a few other potential benefits that you could relate to support your request for a meeting.

Select a time to call that you believe would be agreeable to the prospect. This may be difficult to determine since different people prefer different times to take calls of this nature. Some salespeople believe in calling the prospect's secretary ahead of time to get this information. They say it shows consideration to the prospect and makes the secretary feel important, thus paving the way for the sales call. Other experienced salespeople suggest calling before or after regular hours when you have a good chance of talking directly to the prospect. Generally, the first regular working hour of the day is a poor time to call because the prospect is busy facing the first crisis of the day, attending a meeting, reading her mail, or making her own calls.

How do you feel about the calls you receive from salespeople or other businesspeople, including your clients? Do they show respect for your time? If you have any pet peeves, be sure you don't repeat someone else's mistakes. When you make a telephone call to a prospective client, you take up that person's time, so show the respect you would expect to get if your positions were reversed.

Prepare yourself for the call by getting all needed material in front of you—don't interrupt the conversation to hunt for it. Concentrate on the purpose of the call. Close your mind to other jobs and problems in which you are involved. Try to avoid interruptions at your end. Anticipate some of the objections or tough questions you may get and write down what your response might be. Prepare yourself for resistance and even failure.

In a later chapter we discuss the subject of speaking, but because of the special audio considerations of the telephone, it might be worth making a few points now. As you know, your voice is on its own. The other person cannot see how pleasant or good looking you are nor can he be helped by the gestures you normally use in personal communication to help explain or emphasize your points. So you want to make that voice work for you, not against you. First, be cheerful. The best way to put cheer in your voice is to tell yourself how eager you are to speak to the prospect. Speak with enthusiasm. Project in your voice a degree of excitement about the opportunity that is present. If you have a tendency to speak fast, make an effort to slow down; fast speech can come across as high pressure. Check the volume of your voice. Some people can and do fill a room with their voices, and on the phone this can be tough for the person at the other end. Somehow there is less of a problem for people with soft voices; they can still be heard on the phone. However, mumbling or holding the phone away from your mouth can make it difficult for the other person to hear. If you have any doubt about the quality or effectiveness of your voice, ask someone who regularly speaks with you on the phone.

Now, let's make the call. In this example, we will assume you met the prospect recently and are calling to set up an appointment to discuss an opportunity to provide service to her.

Switchboard
"Good morning, Fairchild Realty."

You
"Good morning, Ms. Fairchild, please."

Switchboard
"Hold please. I'll connect you."

Secretary
"Ms. Fairchild's office."

You
"Ms. Fairchild, please."

Secretary
"Ms. Fairchild is at a meeting. May I take a message?"

You
"Yes, this is Roberta Franklin from (your firm). I met Ms. Fairchild at the Heart Fund meeting last week. I have some information she requested. Would you please have her call me? My number is . . . ."

This is not an unusual conversation and you should have no difficulty in getting the prospect to return the call. The points made in this example are: (1) Let the secretary know where you met the prospect; this helps her to remember you. (2) Tell the secretary the purpose of the call so that she will be more likely to prompt the prospect to return it.

Let's continue with the example. Ms. Fairchild returns the call.

Ms. Fairchild
"Hello, Roberta, this is Jan Fairchild. How are you?"

You
"Fine Jan. How are you? (A few seconds of small talk.) I'll just take a minute of your time. Last Thursday you expressed an interest in knowing some of the pitfalls involved in making an acquisition. I've got some information that I think you should see. I'm going to be visiting a client in your area Wednesday. Could I drop by to see you sometime in the afternoon?"

Ms. Fairchild
"Well, . . . let me see . . . . Sure. How about 3 o'clock? . . . Good, see you then."

Not a difficult sale. You got the appointment, which was the purpose of the phone call. The call was easy because the prospect and the CPA knew each other and because the prospect had expressed an interest in the potential service. In the subsequent meeting, they can discuss more directly the value of the services to the prospect. As pointed out in Chapter 1, selling professional services is predicated on the belief that each potential client has *unique* needs and problems and that the CPA/consultant must first determine these before offering solutions or benefits that could fit a variety of customers.

Now let's consider the "cold call"—the selling method in which the salesperson calls a prospect he has not met and tries to sell his product or service. Depending on the type of product or service, the sale could be made on the phone or at a subsequent meeting. What makes the cold call particularly applicable to selling *other* than professional services is the emphasis on talking about a particular feature or benefit that the salesperson believes will fit the needs of any prospect. In short, the product or service sells itself.

Conversely, selling professional services does not easily lend itself to the cold call. Traditional services like audit, tax advice, and management consulting depend on knowing the prospect's business, understanding her unique needs and problems, and then adapting the firm's approach to solve those problems or providing benefits specific to that particular prospect. You cannot possibly go through this process during a cold call, even if you know the prospect.

Changes are occurring in the accounting profession. In the last few years, accounting firms have started to develop products and services that have very definite and fairly uniform features that could benefit a variety of clients. Among these are computer software packages and training programs. Although these products still require the accountant's commitment and skill in their application, they can be sold on their own merits more than any previous services provided by accounting firms. These products, therefore, provide the opportunity to use the cold call as a legitimate and viable selling tool.

The cold call does not generally get as positive a reception as does the follow-up call, which is understandable considering that the cold call is unexpected. You will often need to work around "screeners" and "blockers" to get to the decision maker. When you reach the decision maker, you must be able to convince him to grant you an appointment.

Let's see how to get past the screener. In this example, you are selling a computer software package for financial planning. You have not met the prospect, but you have done research on her company, and you believe there could be a need for your product. We pick up the conversation as your call is transferred to her secretary.

Secretary
"Ms. Minelli's office."

You
"Ms. Minelli, please."

Secretary
"May I ask who's calling?"

You
"Yes, this is Jim Howell from (your firm)."

Secretary
"Ms. Minelli is not available at the moment. Can you tell me the purpose of your call?"

You
"Certainly. My firm has developed a financial modeling computer program that has particular application for the food processing business. Ms. Minelli would want to know more about that, wouldn't she?"

Secretary
"Perhaps."

You

"I would appreciate it if you would relay that information to her and ask her to call me. Or, would you prefer to have me call again later?"

Secretary

"No. I'll give her the message."

You

"Fine. My number is . . . . I appreciate your help. May I have your name please? . . . Thank you."

In this example, it was important to get the cooperation of the secretary by not refusing her request for information. She was probably told to do this by her boss. Also, it gave her a feeling of being part of the business transaction. The information was presented by you in the form of a benefit, matching the computer program to the food processing business. The statement was followed by a question to the secretary designed to get her to acknowledge that Ms. Minelli could benefit from the program. Although her response, "Perhaps," was not the strongest, she could hardly say no. The question as to whether Ms. Minelli would call back or you should call again was designed to get some action, one way or the other. Your final statement was not only to show your appreciation but also to keep her involved by asking her name.

Getting past the screener requires you to be assertive but also respectful of that person's need to do his job and maintain a feeling of importance. It is a sensitive selling situation, requiring quick thinking and a lot of tact. In this example the screener was the secretary. Other times it could be an associate of the prospect. Each case will determine the exact words you choose to use.

You have created enough interest for Ms. Minelli to return your call. Let's pick up the conversation.

You

"Hello, Ms. Minelli. Thank you for returning my call. I'll only take a moment of your time. I read in *Food Processing* last week about the need your industry has for getting better management information. Would I be correct in assuming your company shares the need?"

Ms. Minelli

"Well yes, we have discussed that."

You

"Our firm has developed a financial modeling computer program that produces consolidated financial statements, budgets, inventory projections, cash flow projections, and other applications. Do any of these hold interest for you?"

Ms. Minelli

"All of them do to some extent."

You

"Perhaps we could discuss the program in a little more detail and see how it could help you. May I come to your office?"

Ms. Minelli

"Frankly, Mr. Howell, you are the third person to call me in the past 2 weeks with the same type of product. I really don't have the time right now to discuss it. Why don't you send me some literature?"

You

"Well, I could do that, but I think it might give you too general a picture. Is this the time you do your projections for next year?"

Ms. Minelli

"Yes, and that's the main reason why I don't have time to talk to anyone. Preparing projections is a big job and requires a long time to get them right."

You

"I can appreciate that. Many business people face that problem. Ms. Minelli, our projection applications have been designed especially to deal with the very problems you are wrestling with. I know how busy you are, but this might be the best time for you to see our program when there is an immediate application with something you are working on."

Ms. Minelli

"All right. But only 20 minutes. Let's see . . . how about Thursday of next week at 8:00 a.m.?"

You

"Fine. I'll see you then. Bye."

In this case, you did not get through to the prospect on your initial call but created enough interest to have her call back. If she had come to the phone when you originally called, you would have pursued the same conversation.

For the cold call to succeed, you must follow the same guidelines as those for the follow-up call plus a few others. You must know your product very well, do your homework as to the needs of the company you are calling, and correctly identify the person who can grant you the interview. This could be the decision maker or someone who could influence the decision maker. When making a cold call, you must particularly respect the time of the person you are calling. Often you will be interrupting them when they are involved in something important, and they may show their annoyance. This will require a great deal of tact and understanding on your part. And you must be *brief*. Despite a cool and sometimes belligerent reception you must be persistent in pursuing the agreement for an appointment. The best way to do this is to follow a loosely structured sequence of steps similar to those in the example just given. (Many of the points in these steps will be explained in depth later in the book.) The following is a run down of the sequence of steps.

1. Open your conversation with a statement or question aimed at getting your prospect's favorable attention.
2. Ask the prospect if this is a convenient time to talk, adding that you will take only a couple of minutes.
3. Tell the prospect one general benefit about your product that will be of interest to him.
4. If you get a favorable response, request an appointment.
5. If you do not succeed in your request, probe for a more specific need.
6. If the prospect acknowledges the need, request an appointment. If the response is not receptive, be prepared to counter objections. Then, if successful, request an appointment.
7. If the prospect agrees, acknowledge the appointment and close the conversation.

If, despite everything you say, you cannot get an appointment, then you should graciously close the conversation, thanking the prospect for her time. If you still feel you have a potential prospect, follow your call a few days later with a note expressing your appreciation for the time she spent and enclose some information that would be of specific interest.

Calling for appointments is not an easy job, and it is sometimes frustrating. Yet, what choice do you have? Wait for the prospect to call you? Hope for referrals? Those opportunities will still occur, but with decreasing frequency. As your firm and others continue to develop and compete for clients by introducing new products, those of you who have the drive and skill to pick up the phone and contact prospects will have a distinct advantage over your competition.

We are ready now to examine in Chapter 5 the rather intensive preparation that is needed for your next meeting. This is the one step that salespeople shy away from most, yet those that are willing to do the necessary work are the most consistent winners.

SKILL-BUILDING TECHNIQUES

1. Select one prospective client whom you would like to know better. Arrange to meet this person at a place he frequents in his business, his social life, or his community activity. Initiate a conversation and gradually move from social subjects to discussion about his business. Tactfully probe for a problem, concern, or opportunity he may have. Demonstrate your interest and ability by offering some insight into the particular subject. If appropriate, try to arrange a meeting in which you can discuss the subject more fully. At the very least, call the prospect within one week to provide him with additional information about the subject.
2. Make a follow-up call to someone you have previously met who had discussed aspects of her business that might be helped by your services. Provide that person with additional information about the subject she discussed with you.
3. If you're feeling brave and you've got something to sell and you know who might be able to use it, make a cold call to get an appointment.

Chapter Five

Preparing for the Sales Meeting

Congratulations! At that initial contact you demonstrated sufficient interest and expertise that you were able to arrange a meeting at which you and the prospect can explore more fully what you can do to serve his organization. You've accomplished your first objective, getting the follow-up meeting. Now, how do you prepare to make that meeting successful?

RESEARCH YOUR PROSPECT'S NEEDS

The success of the meeting will depend largely on your ability to fulfill the prospect's perceived needs. This was discussed in depth in Chapter 3. In addition, you want to feel confident at that meeting, and you want your confidence to show—this requires the right kind of preparation, as the following comments from a colleague illustrate:

You're damn right I prepare for that meeting. I want to feel comfort-
able and look good. I don't mean coming across cocky or arrogant, but
I do want to project confidence in who I am, what I know, and what I
can do for the prospect, and that means doing my homework.

Doing your homework can be an extensive and time consuming job. Therefore, you must be selective in determining what you need to learn before attending the meeting. Obviously, you could dig for innumerable questions, facts, and related information and still not know it all. You need to reduce the research to a manageable task.

The 4-P Formula

Put yourself in the shoes of the prospect. What is on her mind? What are her business and personal goals? What problems is she wrestling with? What would she like her business to look like in 2, 5, or 10 years? What would this mean to her?

These questions could be grouped into four major categories—the four *P*s: what you need to know about the prospect's *product* or business, what you need to know about him as a *person*, what you need to know about his *problems*, and what his *payoff* would be if his problems were solved.

What about the product? Most accountants like to see themselves as business advisers, able to understand their client's business and conducting their service accordingly—a noble objective. It is doubtful, however, that most accountants actually fulfill this role in the eyes of their client; this is one reason why so many businesspeople retain the stereotyped image of the public accountant. One CPA had this complaint:

It really bugs me to have people see us in such a limited role. We've
come a long way from that image, and I don't like to hear someone
refer to us, even jokingly, as mounds of ice, wrapped in 14-column
paper, looking from beneath green eyeshades.

Undoubtedly, this image is, for the most part, inaccurate and unfair. Yet for some people it persists and will change only if we do something to change it. One way is to be able to talk intelligently about the prospect's business: what it is, how it operates, and what it hopes to accomplish. This does not mean that we need to be experts about every aspect of the business, but we should be prepared to ask a few questions or make some comments on a variety of subjects when we are meeting with the prospect. One colleague put it this way:

I try to find out everything I can about the prospect's industy or business. The chances are he's not a CPA, and even if he does have an accounting background, he probably has a lot of other business interests. I really don't think he wants to discuss in detail our audit approach. Hell, if that's all he wants to know, I don't have much to prepare for.

If your prospect is a manufacturer, you may be able to arrange a visit to the plant prior to your scheduled meeting. If you can, you'll probably want to follow the production flow from receipt of raw materials, through work in process, to the shipping of finished goods. This is a good time to observe the manufacturing operation and ask questions of the plant personnel. Do this tactfully so that they don't think you're an efficiency expert or, worse yet, a spy from headquarters. Most plant visits will generate at least three or four subjects that will be of interest to the prospect, and she'll appreciate the time you spent to get to know her business.

Sometimes, the prospect is in a business in which your firm or you has little experience. Then you will need to conduct a crash program which means reading as much as you can and talking to anyone who can help bring you up to speed. You can also count on your experience and knowledge from a related business. True, businesses differ, but there are also many similarities.

Here are some of the business-related questions and issues you might want to be prepared to discuss with your prospect at the initial meeting:

- History of the business
- Principal products or services
- Position in the industry
- Latest technology
- Locations of plants and offices
- Labor situation
- Government regulations
- Marketing process
- Manufacturing or operating process
- Major customers
- Financial results
- Special tax implications
- Major expenditures and costs
- Important ratios

Undoubtedly, this list can go on further. Select those questions and issues that are *most* important for your particular prospect and meeting. Again, don't worry about being an expert on every aspect of every prospect's business. You cannot be, nor are you expected to be, but you do need to show an awareness of something other than just your audit or tax approach. Think like a businessperson and you'll be perceived as one.

Now for the second *P*. What would you want to know about the prospect as a person? Why would you want to know this? Starting with the second question, a CPA had this to say:

I try to find out as much as possible about the person or persons I'm going to meet with. You know, most every serious business need or problem will have some impact on somebody's individual goals, aspirations, and personal interests. If I can find out enough about that person to connect a business problem to a personal need of his, then I'm dealing with powerful material.

Unfortunately, I find this one of the toughest things to do, partly because the personal information is not easily accessible and, second, it takes pretty clear thinking to make this connection.

That's a pretty strong endorsement for wanting to know as much as you can about your prospect. Think about your prospects. What do you know about their personal goals, motivations, and interests? If you think you haven't had time to get this information, then first ask yourself what you know about your present clients. What are they looking to achieve for themselves from their work? If you can't answer this about your present clients, you're missing very important information, and you may eventually be in danger of losing those clients to a more perceptive rival.

Sure, it's tough to find out this kind of information about someone you've only met a couple of times, but it can pay off, as this story illustrates:

I had met Frank only a couple of times before he agreed to meet with me to discuss his estate planning. I assumed that his major reason and motivation was to provide for his wife and two teenage children. In talking to a banker friend of mine who knew him, I learned that Frank had been previously married and had a 20-year-old daughter from his first marriage who lived in Europe and whom he rarely saw. He was very fond of her and was concerned for her future. At the meeting I was able to get him to discuss her, and his concern for her became the focal point of our discussion and the eventual service we were able to provide.

You auditors will say, "Well it's easy for tax people to use this personal information, but how can we use it to sell an audit? An audit is pretty straightforward." You're right. It is easier to use personal information for selling tax services, but in a later chapter we'll see how we can make the connection for audits and other services.

Like most of us, you probably find communicating with some people easier than with others. Somehow, with some people, words come easily, and there is a worthwhile and enjoyable exchange of ideas and information. For others, it is a task, and agreement is difficult to achieve. Yet, the subject is the same as with those with whom we're more successful. Why is this? One reason may be that different people have different communication styles. They speak a different language from us, and unless we can bridge that language gap, we're in trouble. One CPA approaches the problem of style this way:

I want to get to know the communication style of the person I'm going to meet with. I'm one of those typical urgent types who wants to move things quickly and come to fast decisions. You know, bottom-line oriented. But, sometimes I'm with more theoretical or creative types and I have to slow down and adapt to them. How do I find out their communication style? Well, most of the time I've met them before, and I've reviewed my notes and begun to think about their style versus mine. Then, I begin to think how I can adjust my style to theirs.

You may find it helpful to reflect on your own communication style. If you are not sure, ask someone who knows you well, a business associate, your boss, a friend, or a member of your family. Then think about the styles of your clients. With which ones do you communicate best? Less effectively? Why? After this insight, you will find it helpful to explore these questions with your prospects. They are the same as your clients. You just do not know them as well as your clients yet. If you would like to learn more about the subject of communication style, a number of management education organizations can provide training for you.

OK, what else do you want to know about the person or people with whom you'll be meeting? Hopefully, one of the people will be the decision maker—not that you will necessarily expect a decision at the initial meeting, but it's nice to know that the person who eventually hires you will be there to talk with you. If he is, you certainly want to know as much as possible about him, his goals, his interests, and his communication style. Unfortunately, it's not always easy to know if the decision maker will be at your meeting. Don't worry. If he isn't, you'll eventually get to meet him, provided that you do well at your initial meeting. In a later chapter, we'll discuss how to direct the conversation to the decision maker and, perhaps more important, to those we call *powers of influence*.

The third *P* represents an understanding of the client's *problems*, those issues that deeply concern him or her. Certainly, every executive is faced with any number of problems on a given day. Most are dealt with in the ordinary course of the business and pass through without much consequence, but some are of greater concern—the problems that keep her up at night or, at the very least, the ones she thinks about before going to sleep and upon waking up the next morning. One CPA put it this way:

I try to determine what his major problems are, what he's really concerned about. More often than not, he won't tell you what they are. He may not know you well enough to share them with you. So I probe around, speak to other people in the industry who may have similar problems, read trade journals, read articles, and do other research.

Right now, you may be wondering, "Is this guy crazy? How can I possibly spend so much time getting all this information when I have so much else to do. Who is going to do my job if I have to dig up all these data?" You're right. This process can be a lot of work—maybe more than you can handle—but you certainly can do some of it. And if you're fortunate enough to have some help, you can delegate much of this information gathering to others. Have a less experienced accountant do it—it will be valuable experience—or assign it to secretaries or administrative people. With guidance, they will do a good job, and, in addition, they will get a feeling of fulfillment from doing something worthwhile.

The fourth *P* involves understanding what the *payoff* will be to the prospect if her problem is solved. The payoff is the benefit she receives from having her problem solved. For example, a prospect may be having serious difficulty paying bills because of an inadequate cash flow. If she could solve that cash flow problem, she would have more money sooner to pay bills, maintain her credit line, and achieve greater peace of mind. That's a payoff. As the following comment illustrates, understanding the payoff is foreseeing the positive results of solving a problem:

I've always prided myself on being a problem solver, somebody who can dig out the state of concern or unhappiness and figure out the best possible solution. I used to take it for granted that the solution would make things better for the client. Now, I'm more aware from the beginning not only of the problem or state of concern but, specifically,

how the client's life will improve when the problem is solved. It's im-
portant to understand and visualize the desired condition and how
that will affect the client or prospect's life.

Understanding the prospect's problem and payoff is the first step. Being able to articulate that to him is just as important and will be covered in a later chapter. Also, keep in mind that it is doubtful that you will be able to find out everything you want before your meeting, but you'll have a chance to acquire additional information at the meeting itself. To summarize, the 4-P formula calls for an understanding of your prospective client's *product, personality, problems, and payoff.*

THE CPA CONNECTION

Most professionals can appreciate the benefit of following the 4-P formula in researching their prospects. It gives them specific information that gets to the heart of the buying decision. What is less discernible is how this information, particularly motivational needs, is connected to the services that the professional has to offer. For example, what is the connection between a prospect's need for power and a firm's audit services? The two seem miles apart. Before making that connection, let's try a couple of simpler examples from other businesses. For instance, a person has a strong motivational need for status and fulfills this need by buying a Porsche automobile; another person has an equally strong motivational need for security, resulting in that person's decision to invest only in government bonds. Figure 5-1 shows the connection.

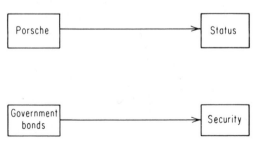

FIG. 5-1. *Examples of need fulfillment.*

In these examples, the connection is direct and easy for the salesperson to see. This in turn makes the buying decision less complex. However, in selling professional services, the connection is not always obvious. You need to think through a *sequence* of steps that will connect the prospect's motivational need with your service.

1. Determine what the prospect would have to do within his or her organization in order to satisfy business and personal goals.
2. Determine whether your firm has both the capability and the willingness to help the prospect achieve these goals, especially if they are personal and not business goals.
3. Determine the point or points at which your firm's capabilities and the prospect's goals can be linked. This common ground represents the CPA connection.

To create a hypothetical example, let's say our prospect is the vice president of finance of a large multinational chemical company and his strongest motivational need is power. We are looking to provide the company with audit services. Beginning with his need for power, we would diagram the initial situation as shown in Fig. 5-2.

FIG. 5-2. *Example of unfulfilled need.*

One way for the prospect to get power is to gain greater control over the company's foreign operating units. He can achieve this through (1) administering the financial and budgetary operations and (2) making a critical analysis of the foreign units' operations. To get control over the financial and budgetary operations, he will need the approval and support of top management. In our capacity, we cannot directly help achieve this. However, to conduct a critical analysis of the foreign units' operations he will need reliable management and financial information. In Fig. 5-3 we add that information to the diagram to indicate how the power base is established.

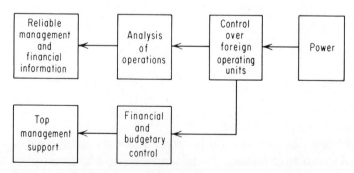

FIG. 5-3. *Establishing a power base.*

To make this power base work, he will need an accounting firm's integrated service approach. This would include three important resources: (1) expertise in the chemicals industry, (2) a worldwide network to serve their various locations, and (3) value-added services that include foreign accounting expertise, tax planning for the company and key personnel, and systems capability to help them with their design of financial and budgetary controls, and the consolidation of management and financial information. Figure 5-4 shows the completed diagram describing our hypothetical firm's services and how they can be seen to connect to the prospect's need for power.

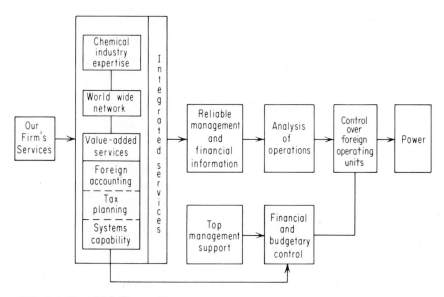

FIG. 5-4. The CPA Connection.

This is a good exercise to go through after you have completed most of your research and are starting to think about how you can begin to introduce your firm's services. All you need is a pencil, paper, and the ability to see a logical sequence of activities.

SOURCES FOR RESEARCH

The next logical question to ask is where to get this information about product, person, problems, and payoffs. Much of it can be picked up from the newspapers and national business magazines. The better ones report the highlights of what is currently happening in a way that can be understood without being an expert in that business. For more technical input and inside data, skim through the trade journals dealing with the prospect's business and industry. If you have access to a business library, have them do a search for the most current happenings. Read Dun & Bradstreet reports or other sources that may give you a clue as to the company's health and other aspects of your prospect's business. Talk to people who know the prospect or are familiar with his business. These people could be bankers, lawyers, business writers, community leaders, or friends you have in common. You may also gain important information from the prospect's competitors, employees, or people he does business with. Of course, this must be done tactfully and confidentially.

Still another source of information can be tapped in preparation for the meeting. The CPA quoted here suggests calling the prospect a few days before the meeting to ask him what he would like to discuss:

It's not enough for me to be prepared to talk about what I think should be covered at the meeting. I want to be sure that we accomplish his goals, too. So I'll call a few days before the meeting and ask him if there are any particular points he wants to cover. Most of the time he doesn't have too much to suggest that I haven't already thought of, but once in a while, he'll mention something that's important to him that I hadn't considered. I recall one time that I was preparing for a meeting in which we were to talk primarily about our approach to an audit. When I called to discuss the agenda, he said that he had just been contacted by someone interested in possibly buying him out, and could we discuss that subject at the meeting.

An obvious benefit to calling to discuss the meeting agenda is that you demonstrate your interest in what is important to the prospect. That is bound to help the prospect see you as an adviser and helper and not just a seller of services.

PLANNING THE MEETING

Having acquired as much information as you can in preparation for the meeting, your next step is to plan your strategy for the meeting.

To begin, you should know how long the meeting is planned for, and this could have been decided during the call to discuss the agenda. When you've determined the length of the meeting, go through all your information and try to decide what questions still need to be answered, allowing sufficient time for this at the beginning of the meeting. Next determine what major issues you want to discuss and how you or your firm might be of help. This CPA explains his technique for this purpose:

I have a little exercise I go through prior to the meeting. I take a piece of paper and divide it into four columns. The first column is headed "Prospects, Needs, or Concerns," the second "What Our Capability Is," the third "The Related Benefits to the Prospect," and the fourth any "Evidence" I can think of to support the benefit I say he will get. I list the first need or problem, then go across the sheet completing the other three steps. Then, I list the second need, and so on. By the time I've completed that sheet, I've got a pretty good idea of what I want to cover at the meeting and it's done in selling terms, not just a lot of descriptive information.

Keep in mind that this is a worksheet that represents your best guess of what is important to discuss but that it is subject to change at the meeting if your questions reveal additional important issues. Having completed your worksheet, you will probably need to pare it down to emphasize the important issues to fit within the time limit of the meeting.

Next, try to determine who will be at the meeting from the prospect's side. Often, she will bring in her controller or other financial people. Know as much about them as you can. Although they may not be decision makers, they often represent what we call *powers of influence* and can either help or hurt your cause. A power of influence can be another member of the prospect's organization or someone from the outside, such as an attorney, banker, or member of the board of directors, who has a strong influence over the decision maker.

Having determined who will be present from the prospect's side, you can then better decide who, if anybody, you will bring with you to the meeting. Usually, you will want to have a fairly equal number from each side, but if the prospect has a couple more, that's fine. More important, you don't want to have six people to her two.

Generally, bring whoever can contribute to the meeting. For example, the prospect, particularly the financial person, will want to meet the person who will run the job and work directly with his people. You may wish to bring a tax person if the prospect has a strong need or interest in taxes. When making a proposal to a very important client, the prospect may want to meet the partner in charge of the office or, on still rarer occasions, a senior partner from the executive or home office. Remember that most business executives are not really impressed with a parade of your ranking partners located halfway across the country. They would much rather meet those people with whom they are going to have a day-to-day communication and working relationship.

It won't hurt to rehearse this material. If you are expected to make a more formal stand-up presentation, then rehearsals are mandatory. (Some accounting firms have professionals in their organization who offer advice on strategy, presentation techniques, and use videotape to help prepare the presenters.)

If your presentation requires audiovisual equipment, slides, overhead transparencies, film, or videotape, be sure your visuals are well done—not necessarily super slick (that fools no one), but rather visual materials that are clear and make their point. If you do not have an audiovisual person in your firm, find a consultant or take the time to find out how to do a good job yourself. Otherwise, you can end up with a disaster, as happened in this story:

It was a horrible meeting. I told the senior accountant to prepare some overhead transparencies showing important information from the prospect's financial statements. Foolishly, I didn't review them before the meeting. When we showed the information, it couldn't be seen. The senior had reduced and copied the entire financial statement on the transparency. There must have been thirty lines of data jammed together. It was very embarrassing.

One more suggestion on using audiovisual equipment is to make sure you know how to use it and provide for extra bulbs and other unexpected contingencies. If you are meeting at the prospect's office, be sure he has adequate space to handle your presentation. It is advisable to let him know you intend to use audiovisual equipment.

CHOOSING THE RIGHT TIME AND PLACE

What time of day do you want to hold the meeting? Unless there is only one choice available or there is a tremendous rush to have the meeting, you will probably have a few options. Some options are better than others, and there is nothing wrong with turning down less desirable times until you get the one you want. You may take the initiative and give the prospect two or three options to choose from.

Some people function better earlier in the day; others are more effective later. If the prospect in some way lets you know her preference, it probably makes sense to accommodate her. However, most executives conduct their business in the traditional daily time frame and usually will respond better during certain predictable times. Morning is generally best. One CPA gives these reasons:

I try for the 9:30 or 10:00 a.m. hour. It's early enough for my prospect to still be fresh but not too early if he's a "night owl" who takes a while in the morning to wake up. Also, it gives him a chance to read his mail or handle important issues that can't wait. I plan for the initial meeting to go no longer than an hour. This means I'm finished by eleven o'clock and I don't have to worry about that awkward lunch hour. If the meeting is planned to end after 11:30, then I'll make it clear that I must leave at that time for another appointment.

The second time option is to hold the meeting in the afternoon. If your prospect is one who skips lunch or "grabs a bite," then you are pretty safe holding the meeting any time in the afternoon. However, if he is the two-hour, two-martini luncher, then he may need a half-hour digestion period to get his attention back to you.

With rare exceptions, any time after 3:30 will be nonproductive. Executives, like doctors, sometimes fall further behind on their appointments as the day goes by, and your afternoon appointment could wind up at the end of the day, when the prospect is tired and disinterested in what you have to say.

A third option is to hold your initial meeting over lunch. We are not about to invite the ire of business lunch devotees by ruling this option out, but there appear to be more reasons against than for holding the meeting over lunch. Let us examine the pros and cons.

A business lunch is best with someone with whom you already have a business relationship. It can provide a change of pace in an environment where more personal discussions may be held, where two-way communication can easily be shared in a conversational mode. It can be a pleasant oasis from what might so far have been a difficult day for the prospect or you, and there are no interruptions from telephones or other people in the prospect's office.

However, holding your initial meeting over lunch takes time. You have to decide what place is appropriate, something that is agreeable to both you and the prospect, especially the prospect. In some cities, even with reservations you may have to wait for a table, and if it is a good restaurant, it will probably be crowded and that adds more time. Unless you are a steady supporter of a restaurant, with your special table, you may find yourself surrounded by other noisy diners, making conversation a real challenge. You may be seated in a direct path with the kitchen, constantly jostled by hurrying waiters and dish carriers. Some restaurants are not large and noisy. They are small and intimate, so intimate that the distance between tables is no more than 12 inches and your personal business discussion can be heard by other parties sitting next to you.

Some of these evils can be avoided by going to a private club where there is generally more space and privacy, provided that the food is good and you do not have to travel too far to get there. Even so, some view the club with mixed feelings:

I used to always take prospective clients to the club for lunch. The staff knew me, and I always got a good table. Then one day I was with Fred, discussing the possibility of doing a businessman's review for his company. Suddenly he looked up, gave a sickly smile, and weakly waved his hand. I turned around; it was his accountant, who knew me. Fred was obviously embarrassed and our discussion didn't go anywhere. I know the same thing could happen at a restaurant, but at least the chances are not so great as at a club where a lot of professional people come for lunch.

Perhaps the strongest reason against conducting an initial sales meeting at lunch is that food gets in the way. At an initial meeting, you want to ask a lot of questions to gather needed information. This means the prospect will do most of the talking while you do most of the listening and eating. Finally, he gets around to eating his cold food long after the waiter has removed your plate. Of course, you can be polite and let your food get cold, too.

How about drinks at lunch? That is a pretty personal issue. Some people drink alcohol at lunch, some do not. Certainly, the restaurant would like you to. Alcohol can relax people and make lunch an enjoyable experience. However, it probably does not add to the sharpness of the business discussion and in some cases can be a negative factor.

Business lunches can be enjoyable and beneficial, particularly when you know the other person well and the subject is discussed informally, but when you want to gather information or discuss a subject in depth, it's better to talk business in a business setting.

In summary, the critical rules for preparing for that all-important sales meeting are:

- *Do not* shortcut; take the time to plan carefully.
- *Do not* allow another client crisis to interfere with your preparation.
- *Do not* attempt to "wing it" because you are knowledgeable and articulate.
- *Do your homework.* You may not get another chance.

In the next chapter, you will start using some of this hard-earned information as you begin your meeting.

SKILL-BUILDING TECHNIQUES

1. Prepare for your meeting with a prospect (perhaps the one from your assignment in Chapter 3) by researching what you need to know about the prospect's product or business, the prospect as a person, existing problems, and the payoff if the problems were solved. Use the following planning worksheet.
2. Construct the "CPA connection" for your prospect similar to the example used in this chapter. Remember to start with your prospect's primary motivation and work backward to your service.

PROSPECT RECORD

Company _____ Address _____

Tel.# _____ #Empl. _____ Volume _____ Profit _____

Accountants _____ Bankers _____

Other advisers _____

Key personnel _____

_____

Describe company (industry, products, operation, financials, etc.).

_____

_____

_____

_____

_____

_____

_____

_____

_____

_____

_____

Describe key personnel (position, responsibilities, goals, needs, interests, etc.).

_____

_____

_____

_____

_____

_____

_____

_____

_____

_____

_____

Describe company problems and opportunities.

_____

_____

_____

_____

_____

_____

_____

_____

_____

Describe how key personnel will benefit from problems being solved.

_____

_____

_____

_____

_____

_____

_____

_____

_____

_____

Other information.

_____

_____

_____

_____

_____

_____

_____

_____

_____

_____

CONTACT RECORD

Results of meetings, phone calls, mail, other communication

Date	

Chapter Six
Starting the Meeting

You wake up on the morning of your meeting fresh and ready to go. No? Well, maybe staying up late last night was not such a good idea! Some people can get by on just a few hours sleep and be full of energy the next morning, but most do better with a full night's rest before going the next day to an important presentation.

Sometimes though, despite our best efforts to get that rest, we just cannot sleep the night before, as with this colleague:

When I have a sales presentation to make, it seems I can never get a full night's sleep. My mind is reviewing all the questions that can arise, what I'm going to say, and what objections they're going to raise. I'm usually up an hour earlier and my motor is going, and I'm ready to get on with it.

Actually, this feeling of excitement and anticipation is a good sign. It means your body and mind are primed for a major effort. It is similar to that feeling you get right before you are about to give a speech—dry throat, sweaty palms, and queasy stomach. Do not worry about these symptoms; they are positive signals that you are ready to have the meeting.

SETTING THE STAGE

Get to your appointment on time or, better yet, a few minutes early. In some countries it may be the custom to arrive late, but being on time or even arriving early usually can work to your advantage. One consultant who has learned to make effective use of such lead time says:

I try to get to the meeting about 15 minutes early. It gives me a chance to observe the reception room, who walks in, and what's being talked about. I look around and try to get a feel for the decor. That tells me something to comment about when we begin our meeting. I'll open up a conversation with the receptionist or the prospect's secretary. Why? Because I like people, and I want them to remember me as someone who was interested in them.

When you enter the prospect's office, project enthusiasm and confidence. This means using a purposeful stride, a firm handshake, and a warm smile. Although this may seem basic, an amazing number of professionals suddenly lose their professional bearing when they begin a sales call. Everything you say or do should reflect your confidence and interest in helping the prospect.

At this point the prospect will probably offer you a seat. If there is only one chair available, you may not have a choice, but some salespeople try to negotiate a seating arrangement that helps them in their selling, as this example illustrates:

I definitely try to avoid sitting in a sofa or a very soft chair. I remember doing that once, and I was looking up at the prospect for the whole meeting. I really felt uncomfortable and somewhat inferior. Also, when I'm sitting in a sofa or easy chair, I have a tendency to slump, and that interferes with my ability to look, sound, and be alert and enthusiastic. Now, I take a quick look around and begin to head toward a straight-back chair. I've never been turned down yet.

If the meeting is to take place in a conference room around a table, then this problem is avoided, but there are other considerations. The prospect will usually sit at one end of the table, which then becomes the head of the table—do not sit at the other end. The expanse of table will create a physical barrier, and the face-to-face confrontation at that distance may create a psychological barrier as well. Instead, sit at the first chair to the right or left of the prospect. This will allow her to maintain leadership of her "turf," but you will be close enough to establish rapport and easy conversation. If others are at the meeting, it would be best for the prospect's people to sit opposite you so that you are facing them, and for your associate or associates to sit next to you so that they can easily share materials with you as needed.

CLUES TO HELP YOUR APPROACH

Any spare time before your meeting starts can be used to quickly observe your prospect and his or her office. Does the prospect project a particular style that you will want to take into consideration when you present your services?

For example, you may walk into an office that impresses you as very neat and well-organized, with everything in place. The furniture is conservative, technical books are lined up directly at the edge of the shelf, and a calculator is within easy reach. Your prospect looks every bit as orderly and well-groomed, dressed in a perfectly fitted dark suit and neatly shined shoes.

The chances are that this prospect will appreciate a well-organized presentation and will want to be led through a series of logical steps. He will probably want to get into the fine details, so be prepared to show schedules and statistics. Present more than one approach. Prospects prefer a few options to compare and choose from.

Or you may walk into an office that has a very warm look, with comfortable furniture that is designed to make the visitor feel welcome. You might see attractive pictures on the wall, plants on shelves and window sills, and family photographs on the prospect's desk. Your host will probably greet you with a warm smile and a firm handshake. He will be wearing comfortable but tasteful clothes. Be prepared for more than the usual small talk, because this is a person who really enjoys getting to know people before the business begins. Since this prospect is strongly oriented toward people, be sure that your questions and answers reflect your interest and concern for others, particularly other members of his organization. Also, describe your firm's services in a way that points out how the members of his organization will benefit from these services.

Another office may strike you immediately as somewhat "different." At first, it may appear strange and disorganized, with abstract pictures on the wall and strange gadgets lying around. A quick glimpse at the bookshelf reveals titles dealing with unusual theories and futuristic concepts. The prospect may be dressed in a mix of styles with no apparent attempt at coordination. This rather offbeat appearance reflects her general disinterest for the mundane, predictable, and orderly life. She would rather deal with imaginative and visionary ideas and let others worry about how the ideas will be implemented. If you are a well-organized person, and many CPAs are, you may feel uncomfortable with this person. But you are going to have to adapt to her style. Leave all those carefully detailed schedules in your briefcase and begin to talk and think like a futurist. Demonstrate your ability to do some blue-sky thinking.

Finally, another office you enter may appear very functional, almost cold, with no unnecessary frills. It will look somewhat disorderly, reflecting the style of someone who works on several jobs at once. You will not see too may books here, probably more digests and journals designed for quick skimming. This prospect is a no-nonsense person who wants results and lives by the bottom line. Be ready to cut the small talk and get right down to business. Stay cool if you are frequently interrupted by the phone. That is this person's style, and he does not consider it a discourtesy. Be direct in your questions, think quickly about your responses and be prepared to describe your services in a way that gets fast and tangible results. This person will respond favorably to suggestions only if they appear workable and relevant to immediate problems and opportunities.

The possibilities for examples are as infinitely varied as the human personality, and of course there are limits to the usefulness of subjective judgments about personality. The point to keep in mind is that a potential client's personal appearance and the appearance of that prospect's environment may provide clues that can help you to make a more effective presentation.

POWERS OF INFLUENCE

The prospect probably will invite other members of her organization or outside advisers to attend the meeting. Chapter 5 identified these people as powers of influence, people who have the ear of the decision maker and can help you or hurt you.

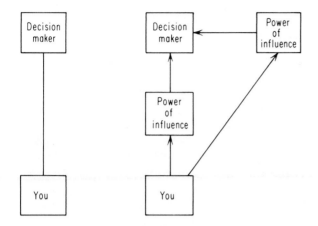

FIG. 6-1. *Direct and indirect paths to decisionmakers.*

Figure 6-1 illustrates how having a direct path to the decision maker differs from working through powers of influence. You should include the powers of influence in every aspect of the sales meeting. Try to make them feel important. Ask them questions and listen carefully to what is important to them; they too have goals and interests they would like to have served. Later, when you are presenting your firm's services, you can aim some of the benefits that you offer at satisfying these people's needs. You may need to sell a power of influence with the same skill as you sell the decision maker. If you fail to do so, you could be in trouble, as the consultant in this excerpt recalls:

I don't think I will ever forget that meeting. We had been invited by this retail chain to make a presentation for the audit. The president, controller, and vice president of operations were present. I had determined from my research that the president was the decision maker, and, therefore, I directed most of my presentation toward him. Throughout the presentation he was very attentive, and at the end he complimented me on my knowledge of their business and his particular goals and interests. Later, when I was informed that we did not get the engagement, I found out that the vice president of operations, whose interests I had never even considered, had for some reason influenced the president not to engage us. From that time on, I try to satisfy some need of every person at a sales meeting.

The powers of influence are not necessarily trying to obstruct your path. They get paid to advise the decision maker about whom to hire, so treat them in a way that will help them choose you instead of someone else. Treat them as another buyer whose needs are to be satisfied.

OPENING THE DISCUSSION

The prospect may wish to plunge right into the purpose of the meeting, which is fine. More often than not, though, an initial small-talk period helps to ease people into the main subject. Be prepared to initiate this conversation with any number of methods. For instance, one CPA does the following:

Generally, I try to open the meeting with some small talk. I do not mean the weather or something especially trite, but perhaps an event that is getting attention in the community or something I noticed as I was walking to his office. What I really want to do is to get his attention off whatever it was on and get it on to me.

Getting the prospect's attention is extremely important. Even though you have an appointment, the prospect has not cancelled all her other business and has not been anxiously waiting for the last 2 hours to see you, as this story proves:

I remember one time I was talking about a particular tax shelter that the prospect was interested in, and he just didn't seem to be listening; he seemed preoccupied. I was really perplexed, because most people are interested in a subject that's going to save them money. Finally, he apologized and said he had been thinking about another problem that had to be resolved right away and would I mind speaking to the controller while he took care of it. Of course I agreed and he called me back in about 15 minutes. For the remainder of the meeting, he was far more relaxed and listened attentively.

Another method for getting your prospect's favorable attention is to begin with a sincere compliment that has to do with him, his business, or some other part of his life. To be sincere, the compliment must be true and expressed with real warmth without going overboard. Try to find something the prospect has not heard too often, perhaps one of the lesser-known achievements of which he is proud, as in the following example.

Jim Patterson operated, without doubt, the best restaurant in town. His food had been praised in a number of magazines and newspapers,

*and people stop him on the street to tell him how much they enjoy
eating at his restaurant. I recall being surprised one night hearing Jim
as the principal speaker at a community function. He spoke on the importance of establishing a Big Brother program for the disadvantaged
young people in the city. I was amazed at how dynamic and excited he
was about the subject. He got a tremendous response from the audience. Some time later I had the chance to talk to Jim about some tax
work. Early in the meeting, rather than making the usual comment
about his restaurant's fine food, I mentioned how impressive he had
been when he spoke that night. His face lit up and he spoke for at least
15 minutes on how he got interested in the Big Brother program and
why he believed so strongly in it.*

Some other ways to break the ice and get the prospect's attention
are to discuss a common interest, mention an article about her business, ask a provocative question, or tell a story that will be of interest.
Remember that small talk is meant to last just long enough to move
gracefully into the purpose of the meeting. Do not let it go on and on.
If necessary, tactfully change the subject to the meeting's purpose.

One of the ways to move into the business purpose of the meeting
is to refer back to your prior meeting and say that you have picked up
some additional material on the subject that you would like to share
with the prospect. Keep this brief; you have other objectives to accomplish before getting too involved in this material.

Much of the information you have about the prospect came
through the research you did prior to the meeting. However, there
will be areas where you will want to acquire more information before
you begin to discuss what your firm can do to help him and his
business. This will require you to ask questions, listen carefully, and
digest what you hear; all of this is the subject of Chapter 7.

SKILL-BUILDING TECHNIQUES

1. Prepare an opening statement or question that will get the prospect's favorable attention at the beginning of your meeting.
2. When you enter the prospect's office, get a quick mental picture of
   the office surroundings, the prospect's appearance, and anything
   else that will give you a clue to his or her personal style.

Chapter Seven
Identifying the Prospect's Real Needs

Earlier we determined that a sale involves a buying decision that is based on the prospect's needs being fulfilled. In Chapter 5, we described the research process for finding out these needs and other information about the prospect. You now have an opportunity at this meeting to confirm much of what you have found out and to pick up new information that will help the selling process. This is done through effective questioning, which includes building a questioning period into your presentation. This chapter discusses:

- Benefits of questioning
- Areas for questioning
- Types of questions
- How to ask questions
- Active listening
- Restatement and reflection
- Note taking

BENEFITS OF QUESTIONING

Here are a few specific benefits of asking the prospect questions:

1. You will confirm information you have already discovered or find out that some of it is incorrect.
2. You will acquire additional information that will help you better understand what the prospect really needs or wants, to identify his "hot button," so to speak.
3. You will become more confident about the outcome of the meeting because you will have more data to work with.
4. You will match the needs you have heard about to what you will say about your services when you move into that part of the presentation.
5. You will get the prospect talking, sometimes a difficult thing to do at the beginning of a sales interview.
6. You will display your interest in the prospect and her organization, a characteristic that must be recognized by the prospect if she is to accept you as one of her business advisers.
7. You will have, perhaps most important, the chance to demonstrate your expertise by the nature of the questions you ask.

Here is how one CPA views the role of questioning in a selling situation.

I used to think that the only way to show how smart I was, was to give people answers to their questions or problems. Then I found out that I could demonstrate my knowledge just as well by asking pertinent questions. I could get the prospect thinking about issues he never thought about before or that his present accountant never asked him. And the best part was that I didn't come across as the big know-it-all with all the answers.

Obviously, skillful questioning is extremely important whether you are an auditor, consultant, or any other kind of professional. To open up the questioning period without coming on like you were investigating a homicide, you may want to say something like, "Jim, to save time and zero in on the issues that are most important to you, would it be all right if I asked you a few questions?" There are no reported cases of a prospect having turned down a request phrased in this way.

AREAS FOR QUESTIONING

Chapter 6 identified four areas for research (the 4-P formula): product (business), person(s), problems, and payoff (to prospect). Use these same areas as you seek additional information in questioning.

At the beginning of the questioning period, the prospect may be a little apprehensive about what you are going to ask, so begin with questions about her business or industry. These subjects are less threatening than questions about her, her people, or her problems. Many business questions can be an extension of what you tried to find out when you were doing your initial research prior to the meeting. A CPA uses the following technique:

I try to get him to analyze his own industry: what he feels are the present major issues and problems and what he sees as the future of the industry. Many industries are directly affected by federal regulations and, particularly, changes in the administration. Most businesspeople don't mind doing a little crystal ball gazing and sharing their opinions with you. Of course, you better be able to contribute something to the conversation, or he's liable to see you as one who has done no preparation.

If you have knowledge and experience in the prospect's industry, exploring the subject can be more of an exchange of information and ideas. If your knowledge and experience is limited, then, obviously, you want the prospect to do most of the talking so that you can learn as much as possible.

After a certain time you will want to direct your questions to the second area, people: those dealing with the prospect's and others' personal needs and goals. Since most businesspeople or executives see their careers as providing a means to satisfy a basic need or achieve a personal goal, getting the prospect to talk freely about this is a major breakthrough.

This is not easy to accomplish. In general, businesspeople do not readily respond to a question like, "Joe, tell me about your personal needs and goals." Instead, you're going to have to arrive at this objective in a more indirect way. Here is one possibility:

George was not exactly the most talkative prospect. Oh, he was friendly and cooperative, but I sensed a reluctance on his part to talk about anything too personal. Then I thought I saw an opportunity and said to him, "George, you've obviously put a lot into this company and are responsible for a large part of its success. I imagine that con-

tributes a lot to what you want to achieve in your life." He looked at me for a moment without speaking, turned away, gazed out the window, and then said, "You know, I've thought about that from time to time, but never really talked about it. I guess this business gives me a feeling of being able to measure my progress in life, what I've been able to accomplish. When I look at the growth in sales and profit, additional facilities I've built, and the number of people working for me, I say, 'George, you're doing good, not great, but better than most of the people you know.' And that recharges my batteries."

Not every question will evoke that kind of personal response, but your success at probing for meaningful information will greatly depend on your ability to conduct an interview in a professional and nonthreatening way.

If your questioning is done skillfully and tactfully, you should be able to lead the prospect into the third area, those questions dealing with the major problems of the business. Some salespeople, professionals included, have difficulty with the idea of confronting prospects with their problems. They believe it will make the prospect uncomfortable and will therefore hurt the chance of making the sale. They therefore neither ask a question nor make a statement that has the potential to make the prospect uncomfortable. However, arousing discomfort in the client is not necessarily bad. The idea is to make the prospect uncomfortable with her present situation so that she will open her mind to the need for change. One professional put it this way:

If I am speaking to a prospect who is basically happy or comfortable with his present situation, he is not going to have much reason to make any big changes in his business and that includes changing his accounting firm. So I use probing questions to see if there are any areas that he should be really concerned about, things he had not thought about, or had not considered that serious. I raise issues that are important to the health of his business, issues that may cause him to flinch a little. Of course, I'm working on the strategy that his present accountants had not brought these issues to his attention. I guess you could say that my objective is for him to question the value of his present accountants and see me as a valuable business adviser who will make him face up to important issues and problems.

This probing can be extremely effective in helping you to discover the prospect's problems and also in helping him to confront them. Of course, you must do this tactfully so he does not become uncomfortable with you. For example, some people are reluctant to share or even admit their problems to people they don't know very well. Saying, "Fran, what are your major problems?" is probably not going to get much of a response. A more acceptable way might be to mention a possible problem in an indirect way. "Fran, I read in the *Wall Street Journal* about the proposed change in regulations in the shipping industry. Does that affect your company in any way?" When the question is phrased this way, the prospect has the option of responding yes or no and of going into whatever depth she feels comfortable with. You hope she will feel comfortable enough to speak at some length about the problem. At this point, you should begin thinking about how your services could help solve that problem. The temptation is to give your answer at this time, but it may make sense to hold off your response until you have more information about other problems. Then you can present your services from an integrated point of view that considers a more complete analysis of the prospect's needs.

The fourth and last area to probe for is the payoff, which, as mentioned in a previous chapter, requires questions that are aimed at finding out what the prospect would like his business to look like when its problems are solved. It is important to get the prospect thinking positively about the future of his business. Here is an experience related by one CPA:

I recall speaking to a prospect about his method for processing customer orders. From my questioning, it became clear that he was unhappy with the lack of accuracy and the length of time it took to process the orders. The problem was clear; it was time to shift my line of questioning. I asked him what his operation would look like if he could solve that problem. His response predictably said that he would be able to ship goods more quickly and bill customers sooner, which would improve his receivable and cash position. That was his payoff, but it was important to get him to say it.

Identifying the payoff lets the prospect see you as one who is focused on positive results. Also, it tells you what to feed back to her when you begin to match her needs with your firm's capability.

TYPES OF QUESTIONS

Having examined the four basic areas of questioning for identifying the prospect's real needs, let's review the general types of questions that you might want to use and how to use them.

Many books have been written about the several types of questions that one can ask in an interview. For selling, you must understand and master three major types of questions.

1. Open-end questions
2. Closed-end questions
3. Probe questions

Each has a specific purpose.

The Open-End Question

The chief purpose of the open-end question is to allow the prospect to think quite a bit about the answer. It provides room for judgment and a variety of responses. An example of an open-end question would be, "How have the new government regulations affected your industry?" Open-end questions often begin with the words "how," "what," "why," and "where."

Since open-end questions can be difficult to frame, inexperienced salespeople usually ask more closed-end questions. Most closed-end questions require only a one- or two-word response, such as yes, no, or another definite answer. One CPA who had trouble with questioning describes the problem this way:

Types of questions? Hell, I was lucky if I asked any questions at all. I was so anxious to talk about my firm's services, I didn't want to waste time asking questions. I guess my early attempts at questioning were what you called closed-end. I remember one situation where it took all of five minutes to ask my questions and get answers from the prospect.

The Closed-End Question

Closed-end questions do have their uses. They identify numerical or definitive information like names, and they can help to control an overtalkative prospect. They can be used as a follow-up to vague responses to open-end questions, and, finally, they can be effective in getting commitment when you attempt to close the sale. Be careful, though, about asking a quick series of closed-end questions. This can make the prospect feel a little nervous and defensive.

The Probe Question

The probe question is used to probe or dig more deeply into an issue. It generally follows an open-end question, although it can follow a closed-end one. Lawyers call this "a line of questioning" when they do it in court. An example of a probe question might be:

1st (open-end) question
"Why do you want to replace the old system?"

Answer
"It just isn't working well."

Probe question
"Can you identify the problems you're encountering?"

A word of caution about the probe question—if too many are used in a series, the prospect may feel he is being cross-examined.

Watch out for leading questions that indicate you have already assumed an answer or that indicate what you would like to hear. Remember, your objective is to gather information, not to put answers into the prospect's mouth. Two examples of leading questions would be (1) "You don't have any trouble getting your operating report each month, do you?" and (2) "I imagine your people have been pretty well trained, haven't they?" Questions that can be answered yes or no generally have little value unless you are looking for a positive or negative confirmation.

QUESTIONING TECHNIQUES

You can ask all the right questions and still not accomplish your purpose if you do not present the questions to the prospect effectively. Here are some guidelines.

Maintain a relaxed style. This creates a comfortable environment that encourages the prospect to respond. Use his name occasionally and smile, but do it sincerely.

Put contrast in your voice and allow for pauses when you speak. Avoid the machine-gun style of asking questions.

Think through your questions so that your intent is clearly understood and does not cause ambiguity. Don't string two or three questions together; this may cause confusion.

Use simple and familiar words. Avoid jargon and technical terms the prospect may not understand or even care to understand, but do not be so basic as to appear condescending. Choose precise and specific language. Stay away from general words (quickly, often, occasionally) and abstract terms (productivity, efficiency, successful, timely) that the prospect may interpret in a way that differs from the one you intended. Be careful about questions that could trigger a negative reaction toward you. Although you want the prospect to open up and share her problems with you, be sure you are not treading on oversensitive ground that causes the prospect to resent your question or regret that she answered it. Also, be tactful about asking questions about other people in the prospect's organization.

As you ask questions, look at the prospect but avoid a fixed stare that could cause embarrassment or tension. Try to interpret his reactions to your questions. Look for head nodding that signifies understanding or a sudden reaction of keen interest. Remember, you are looking for hot buttons, for areas that you want to really probe.

Give the prospect time to respond to your question. Do not jump in immediately with help or another question. If she does not respond after a few seconds, you may then want to rephrase your question or perhaps find out if your question was understood. Repetitious or condescending questions can be a problem, as the following makes clear:

I had this awful habit of interrupting my own conversation with the expression, "Do you understand?" I guess I did it often and without thinking. One day a good friend called it to my attention, saying my favorite expression had become rather annoying to him, that it implied to him that I questioned his intelligence. From that time on I've tried to avoid saying, "Do you understand?" and instead say something like, "Have I made myself clear?"

Watch out for negative reactions, spoken or unspoken. A tense expression on the face of the prospect may mean discomfort or sudden hostility. If he folds his arms and crosses his legs, this may be a defensive posture indicating resistance on his part. Be prepared to switch your line of questioning or, if you think you can handle it, say something like , "I seem to have hit a sensitive point. Would you care to comment on it?"

Be aware of your own body language, too. When the prospect is responding to your questions or volunteering a comment, make sure your body reflects a receptive mood. Nod your head, look at him, and show interest in what you are hearing. Avoid expressions that could be interpreted as lack of interest, disagreement, or disapproval. This tends to turn the prospect off and you will not get him to respond anymore.

Similarly, do not interrupt unless you don't understand what the prospect is saying. In that case, say something like, "Linda, could you stop for a moment. I'm unclear about the point you just made regarding your plans for expansion. Could you tell me specifically in what areas of the country you're considering to expand your operation?"

Sometimes the prospect enjoys talking and goes on and on or goes off on a tangent. It's best to be patient and listen, but sometimes you can regain control of the selling presentation by waiting for the prospect to take a breath and then quickly but tactfully redirecting the conversation with a comment like, "Bill, I've never quite heard it from that point of view. What effect will that have on this year's operation?"

ACTIVE LISTENING

Obviously, it is important for you to be a good listener. Unfortunately, most people, including salespeople, do not listen as well as they could and often forget or misinterpret valuable information. A colleague had this experience:

I have to admit that I used to have a serious problem listening to prospects. I was so busy thinking about what I was going to say that I missed half of what the prospect was saying. It's really embarrassing when you ask a question and the prospect looks at you and says, "I just told you that 5 minutes ago."

Some causes of poor listening are:

- Distractions caused by the prospect's appearance, mannerisms, or speech, particularly if these are unattractive to you.
- Distractions caused by external factors, such as outside noise, temperature, light, and movement.
- The prospect speaking excessively, poorly, or unclearly.
- Letting other subjects crowd your mind.
- Becoming angry or upset with the prospect's view because it disagrees with your own.
- Becoming disinterested because you've heard it all before.

- Thinking of your next question or what comment you want to make.

Listening can be improved, however. Among ways to do this are the following:

- Look at the prospect. This will encourage her to continue talking.
- Sit up and be alert. An overly relaxed position may cause an overly relaxed mind.
- Let the prospect complete his thought. Keep an open mind that permits you to consider new ideas or points of view different from your own.
- Give nonverbal feedback to the prospect by nodding, using questioning looks, or smiling when it is appropriate.

The idea is to avoid a cold, impassive face. Remember, this is a sales presentation, not a poker game.

RESTATEMENT AND REFLECTION

Even careful listening will not always result in clear understanding. At times you may wish to clarify a particular point the prospect has made. You then can use a technique called restatement, which, as it implies, involves restating in your own words what the prospect has just said. For example:

You
"What are your personal tax needs?"

Prospect
"Well, I've been doing a lot of thinking about my family's welfare."

You
"In other words, you'd like to do tax planning that will ensure that your family is taken care of."

This technique can appear unnatural and sound phoney if the restatement is not preceded by good, sincere listening. In such a case, the prospect may feel she is being "techniqued." Restatement works best when it is sincere, relevant, and not overdone.

Another effective interviewing technique is reflection. This occurs when you hear the prospect expressing a certain feeling, often a sensitive one. To draw out the prospect in a supportive manner, feed back in your own words the emotion you think you are hearing. An example of reflection would be:

Prospect
"What will I say to Bill Andrew? He's been my accountant for 22 years."

You
"You're concerned about how he will feel when you tell him you're planning to change accountants."

Reflection can be very effective in bringing to the surface fear, hostility, and other emotions. However, try to avoid the following potential problems:

- If overused, reflection can become trite and boring.
- You can be perceived as playing psychiatrist.
- Bringing emotions to the surface may not always be advisable.

NOTE TAKING

In the process of gathering information, it is important that you retain it. If you have a reliable memory, you can depend on that to a certain extent. But it is beyond the capability of any interviewer to retain all the information obtained during this part of the sales presentation. This particularly applies to retaining numerical information. Therefore, you probably need to take notes. Some guidelines to follow for note taking are:

- Ask permission to take notes, telling the prospect you would like to jot down the essence of her ideas to refresh your memory and ensure their accuracy.
- Don't use a formal-looking document, since it can be intimidating. Instead, use a common notebook or pad of paper.
- Don't record everything that is said word for word, but rather look for the main issues or ideas. Don't write after every comment. Instead, gather a few ideas and write and listen at the same time.
- To avoid an awkward silence while you are writing, periodically comment about what you are recording.
- Keep a relaxed and interested posture when you are taking notes. This in turn will keep the atmosphere relaxed. Be sure to look at the prospect as often as you can.
- Read back factual notes periodically to make sure you have been accurate.

- If you choose to make notes about the prospect (caution advised), be careful what you write. Some people have a talent for reading upside down.
- When the interview is over, and if there is to be another meeting with the prospect, review your notes in detail. Make sure you can understand everything you have written. While reviewing your notes, add any other information you may recall from your discussion.

At the conclusion of this questioning period, you should have a much clearer picture of the prospect's real needs and an idea of how you are going to match these needs to your firm's capability.

SKILL-BUILDING TECHNIQUES

Think through your next meeting with a prospect and determine the kinds of questions you need to ask to identify her or his real needs. Use the questions at the meeting along with the technique of restatement and reflection.

Chapter Eight

Presenting Your Firm's Capability

Now it is your turn to do more of the talking. You will want to select the right things to say and to say them well. This is the "guts" of the presentation, and your objective is to convince the prospect that you can provide him with what he needs.

Unfortunately, many accountants make a tragic mistake at this point. They think that the best way to convince a prospect of their value is to describe solely and in great detail their firm's services, often with little consideration of the prospect's needs.

The following jingle was given several years ago by Hal Bergdahl, manager of dealer sales for Crane Company, Chicago, at the Sales Executive Club of New York.[1] It clearly states (with one or two word changes) what the prospect does *not* need.

---

[1]Quoted in Percy H. Whiting, *The Five Great Rules of Selling*, rev. ed., McGraw-Hill, New York, 1957; Dale Carnegie & Associates, Inc., Garden City, New York, pp. 105-106.

I see that you've spent quite a big wad of dough
To tell me the things you think I should know.
How your firm is so big, so fine and strong;
And your founders had whiskers so handsomely long.

Your techniques are so modern and, oh, so complete,
Your "rep" is so flawless; your staff can't be beat.
Your motto is "Quality—capital "Q"
—No wonder I'm tired of "Your" and of "you"!

So tell me quick, and tell me true
(or else, my love, to hell with you)
Less—how this service came to be;
More—what the darn thing does for me!

No matter what size your firm, this advice makes sense. Build your presentation around the prospect's needs or risk confusing, angering, or putting her to sleep, all undesirable results. Force yourself away from your old, often-used, standard presentation that could be applied to most any type of prospect. Chapter 7 placed so much emphasis on questioning and listening because you must respond to what you heard the prospect say, not what you *think* he should know in regard to your firm's capability.

THE PRESENTATION AS A MATCHING OPERATION

The whole selling experience can be viewed much like a computer operation with you as the computer. The initial information-gathering steps, research and questioning, represent the input of data to you. You have collected a mass of information, probably more than you need. Turn this information over to your central processing unit (CPU) for sorting—you are looking to isolate your prospect's key problems and areas of interest, the subjects that seemed to arouse her most visible reactions. These represent her hot buttons, the problems that may be keeping her up at night. When you have isolated the key issues, your CPU then matches these issues to what your firm can provide. Consider this CPA's observation:

It's a matching job, pure and simple. I match what we've got to what they need. Well, maybe it's not that simple, because if you haven't done your homework or asked the right questions, you're not going to

*know what they need. I remember speaking to _____, who is now a
valued client. In our preliminary meeting, it seemed to me he was
only really interested in (1) getting my personal attention and (2)
keeping a smooth relationship with his employees, both conditions
which were not being met with their present accountants. I was afraid
if I emphasized only those two concerns, it would not be enough.
Well, I took a chance and built my selling around assuring him on
those two points. It worked and he accepted without any objections the
other things I could have stressed, and he never questioned the fee.*

The matching concept is not difficult to understand or accept, but it
is not always easy to translate into words that will be meaningful to
the prospect. Therefore, it is important to develop a framework or
system for articulating what you want to say. This framework has five
parts:

1. State your understanding of the prospect's problem, opportunity,
   interest, or concern.
2. Describe your firm's capability to deal with this as a fact or feature.
3. Give a related benefit of your capability.
4. Provide evidence to support the benefit.
5. Confirm benefits with the prospect.

STATE YOUR UNDERSTANDING OF THE PROBLEM

Let's look at the first item in the above list, stating your understanding of the prospect's major problem or area of interest. Unfortunately,
some CPAs feel uncomfortable in pointing out problems, but, as the
following comment shows, others have learned to deal with it:

*I try to match our capabilities to his needs or problems. Each time I'll
first remind him of that need or problem, and then I'll tell him how
we can help him. Some of our people think it's negative to openly confront a client or prospect with his problem. That's _____! We're not
dealing with children. These are realistic businessmen. They know
they're not doing everything right any more than we are. And, they're
damn glad to have someone level with them.*

Obviously you should not be tactless or unnecessarily critical, but you
should be willing to tell your prospect up front what you believe his
problem is. This will quickly establish a communication that is based

on honesty and directness. Most clients appreciate this approach. Let us start to build this five-part presentation with a simple example: "Bill, as I understand it, one concern you have is you're not getting the kind of advice you need for estate tax planning. Is that correct?" This example concludes the statement of the problem with a question that requests confirmation. If you are on target, you will get some affirmative response from the prospect which permits you to continue. If your statement is not accurate, then your question will give the prospect the opportunity to clear it up and get you back on track.

DESCRIBE YOUR FIRM'S ABILITY TO HELP

Now that you've clearly identified a key issue or problem for your prospect and you've got her agreement, next state your firm's capability to deal with that issue or problem. At this point, you are trying to achieve credibility, so avoid any wild claims or other statements that the prospect will greet with skepticism. For example, saying, "We have the best estate tax planning service," or "We are experts in the banking business," are claims that, in the ears of the prospect, cannot be proved, at least at that moment. Furthermore, these statements can be made by any other firm; who is the prospect to believe? You may be saying to yourself, "But we do have the best estate tax planning service in the city." Maybe so, but truth in selling is not determined by what the seller thinks or says but by what the buyer hears and believes. And most buyers will listen and accept statements that are built on facts or features as opposed to claims. So the statement, "We have the best estate tax planning service," could be rephrased, "We have sixteen people in our tax department, and three of them have had a total of 47 years of estate tax planning with over seventy-five clients." The prospect has now heard a statement about your services that is factual, specific, and clear, expressing qualities that will add to your credibility.

In the above example, we used numbers to support the basic fact about your tax service. You can use any terms that will accurately decribe some feature of your service. You might talk about a particular individual and discuss his or her experience or qualifications, or you could describe the features of a software system that your firm provides. Again, the key factor in stating facts or features about your service is that they be clear and believable.

A word of caution—some CPAs use this opportunity to try to show prospects how much they know, often getting into far more detail than is necessary or desirable. One colleague warns:

I'm pretty careful about how deep I go with my technical descriptions. In consulting, there's a tendency to fall in love with the complexity of the problem. That can be bad, because we've got to be sure the prospect understands what we're talking about. Now, this can be a bit tricky because you don't want to appear condescending by talking in too simple terms. So what you have to do is analyze your prospect or group of prospects to determine their level of knowledge, experience, and interest. Then develop your presentation to fit the situation.

Of course, there will be times when you are talking to a prospect who has a good accounting or financial background and who wants to discuss the more technical aspects of your service. Eventually, he is going to want to know how that technical information can help him or his organization specifically. This brings us to the third step in your presentation, showing the relation between each of your firm's capabilities and a specific benefit for the prospect.

GIVE RELATED BENEFITS TO THE PROSPECT

Facts and features provide credibility, but benefits provide the appeal to your presentation, the part that shows your prospect how what she is getting will help her. Let us look first at a product to demonstrate the point. Suppose you're interested in buying a small office computer. If the salesperson says, "This computer has a green non-glare screen," he or she is stating a fact or feature that you will accept as being true, but you may also think, "So what?" If the salesperson follows this statement by saying, "So it will be easy on your eyes when you're working with those number-crunching tasks like payroll and general ledger," then you can clearly see the benefit to you.

You may say that it is much easier to state benefits for products, which are tangible, than for intangible services like audits, tax work, or management services. Perhaps, but that doesn't let you off the hook. You just have to think a little more about it. Here is how one CPA approaches the problem:

I'll talk about our services in terms of the consequences to the prospect. I don't want to spend a lot of time describing an audit activity to him. Instead, I want to explain the result of that activity in terms of consequences that are either good or bad for him. For example, analytical review can be pretty dry if you try to explain how we do it, but if you talk about the potential saving of audit time, then you've got his interest.

Consider again the example used earlier involving the client's problem of getting estate tax planning. Having told him that we have sixteen people in our tax department and that three of them have had a total of 47 years experience in estate tax planning with over seventy-five clients, we could follow with, "This means you're getting the combined thinking of seasoned professionals who have worked with individuals on estate tax planning situations similar to yours." If you can come up with a better benefit than that, good; you're thinking like a salesperson.

Be careful when stating benefits. Don't get carried away in your enthusiasm and overstate what you can do for the prospect. A benefit should be exciting, but more important, it must be deliverable. One accountant interviewed expressed it this way:

As you know, I'm a pretty enthusiastic person, but I can also be very low key in my presentation. I don't state outlandish benefits. I sort of understate what I'm saying. Of course you can do this if what you're saying is important to the prospect. Do you remember the Volkswagen ad a few years ago? I think it went, "We may not be the fastest car on the road but you'll get an honest 55 mph from us." That phrase "may not be" is a beautiful understatement. In other words, I don't come on like a hurricane, but I don't lack for enthusiasm. In my case, it's a quiet enthusiasm.

However, if you are by nature a low-key person, be careful not to overdo this technique. Remember, there is no substitute for enthusiasm.

We have now completed three parts of the selling process. We have reminded the prospect about her problem or interest; we have stated our ability to deal with the problem; and we have related that ability to a specific benefit the prospect will receive.

PROVIDE EVIDENCE TO SUPPORT BENEFITS

The fourth step is to provide evidence to support the promised benefit. If you've accurately and clearly articulated the first three steps, the prospect should be convinced that you can help him. But sometimes, even if he likes what he's heard, there may be some doubt in his mind; he may wonder, "Can you really do this for me? That benefit sounds almost too good to be true."

This is a natural thought process for the prospect to occasionally go through, and it simply requires you to provide some type of proof or assurance. There are a number of ways to do this.

One way is to give an example of how you provided a similar benefit for another client. Tell it in the form of a story so that your prospect can visualize it in her mind, but keep the story short. For example, using our tax situation, you might say the following: "Recently, we had the opportunity to work closely with one of our clients in his tax planning. His main interest was in reducing the amount of his estate tax so that he could leave more to his children. If I recall, the ultimate savings could be about $75,000."

Another type of evidence is some type of visual exhibit that can graphically illustrate what you can do. One CPA suggests the following:

I'm beginning to use more and more visuals in my presentations. They can explain, support, or emphasize something I'm saying. For example, I'll have a full-year calendar with me in which I'll point out how we plan to accomplish the audit on a monthly basis instead of piling everything into the year end. Clients are not naive. They know when our heavy work period takes place, and none of them wants to be shunted aside. So the visual not only explains how we'll work, but it adds to our commitment in the prospect's mind.

Still another type of evidence is a demonstration of what your services can do. For example, some CPAs are very good at making quick calculations on paper in front of the prospect to demonstrate how they might approach a tax or depreciation problem. Do not confuse this technique with providing a full solution to a complex problem the prospect is wrestling with. That will be tackled after the prospect becomes a client. The demonstration is intended to help the prospect understand how you can provide a promised benefit. Those CPAs who provide management services often are involved in analyzing and recommending types of systems to prospective clients. They have the opportunity to provide evidence by demonstrating software applications or even a piece of equipment.

Another type of reliable evidence is referral from a satisfied client. For example:

Referrals are a good type of evidence, and we've always gotten a number of new clients as a result of referrals from satisfied clients. But

*now I'll tell one of my happier clients that I intend to use him as a
reference. If you've done a good job for your clients, they'll be glad to
do it. The difference between referrals today and what they used to be
is now I go out after them.*

So, evidence in some form can provide the credibility to convince
the prospect that you can provide what you promise. Do you need to
provide evidence after every benefit you state? Obviously not. The
client, through his comments or physical reaction may communicate
his belief to you as you relate the benefits of your service. Still, you
do want to provide evidence when the benefit is impressive or when
you see the prospect looking doubtful.

CONFIRM BENEFITS WITH PROSPECT

The last part of our five-step process is getting confirmation from the
prospect that the benefit is important to her. There are two purposes
to this step. One obviously is that, having gone through the process
of the four previous steps, you would certainly want to know
whether you are on target, whether the benefit is as important to the
prospect as you believe it is. The second purpose is to get the client
used to saying yes, or agreeing with you, so that when the time
comes to close the sale, agreement will be natural, not strange or
traumatic. The actual confirmation statement or question is usually
only one sentence, and the wording can range from mild to very
strong. Continuing with our tax planning example, a strong
confirming question would be, "You do want that kind of tax planning expertise, Bill, don't you?" A medium-strong confirmation
would be, "And I think you'll agree, Bill, that that kind of tax planning expertise would be helpful to you." A mild confirmation would
be, "Bill, what do you think of the value of that kind of tax planning
expertise?"

Salespeople often resent using a confirmation question, because
they feel it puts too much pressure on the prospect. If said in a tactful
way, though, it can move the sale much closer to a successful close.
Obviously, you do not want to use a confirmation after every sales
point, because it would become boring. The idea is to use it periodically, particularly when you want the prospect to acknowledge that
he needs a specific benefit that will really help him.

PUTTING IT ALL TOGETHER

Let us put the five parts into another example so you can see how it comes together, this time using a transition from the previous data-gathering steps.

Salesperson
"Mr. Russell, based on what we've discussed, I believe we can give you the kind of service you're looking for. Let's review some of your major interests and concerns. [Problem] First, you mentioned that you wanted a firm that really understands the fashion apparel business. We can certainly appreciate that need. [Fact] In this city alone our firm has nine apparel clients, some of whom we've had for over 40 years. [Benefit] This means that you'll be working with accountants who understand the problems of the apparel business and what's happening in the industry. Your people won't have to teach our people the business. [Evidence] Here's a list of the people we plan to put on your engagement. Next to their names are the apparel clients they serve and the number of years they've been on those jobs. Paula Jones, the senior on your job, has written a widely acclaimed article about applications of LIFO inventory in the fashions apparel business. [Confirmation] Mr. Russell, won't you agree that we have a pretty good understanding of your business? Second, you said . . ."

That whole dialogue takes about 1 minute to say, and that's about all the time you need. When salespeople cover too much information, they usually become disorganized, confusing, and boring, and the prospect tunes out.

Here are some final guidelines for using the selling steps covered in this chapter.

1. Build the five-step process from the research you did before the meeting and the question period preceding this step. If you did not have the chance to research the prospect before the meeting and there are not to be any subsequent meetings, then you are going to have to build this step during the questioning period of this meeting. It will take careful listening and quick thinking on your part to present it effectively.
2. Select those problems or interest areas that are *most* important to the prospect. Do not overwhelm him with too many issues, some of which are only of minor interest to him. In other words, use a few well-placed rifle shots with heavy impact instead of buckshot sprayed weakly all over the place.
3. Be enthusiastic when you present your firm's capability. Let your voice and your body project that enthusiasm. Lean forward and use contrast in your speech. Watch the prospect carefully when

you present your firm's capability. His facial and body signs will give you clues about how he's responding to each of your selling points. If you're explaining a more complex issue and he looks puzzled, you may want to say something like, "Have I made that clear?" Never, never say, "Do you understand?" or "Do you follow me?" or any other statement that suggests the prospect isn't too quick. No matter how dense the prospect, the responsibility for clarity is always on you, the seller.

5. Use your prospect's name periodically; also use the words "your" and "you," particularly when telling her about the benefits she'll receive. This personalizes your presentation and helps the prospect to feel special.

6. If appropriate, relate more than one benefit to a particular feature of your capability, but be careful that you don't put in so many that it confuses the prospect. Three is about the limit.

7. If you've brought tangible evidence with you (forms, schedules, lists, etc.), have it handy and show it only at the time you're presenting the evidence part of the step. Put it away when you're finished so that it doesn't later become a distraction when you're discussing something else. Respect confidentiality if you use another client's experience as your evidence.

8. Try to complete your five steps uninterrupted. If you're on target and brief, this should be no problem. If you are interrupted in the middle of your step, remember where you were and pick it up later.

9. Pause after completing each step to allow the prospect to digest what you've said or to ask a question.

10. Practice the five steps in the order we've discussed. After you know it cold, you can get fancy and move parts around to fit your style and particular situation.

That's it! A five-part formula for presenting your firm's services to your prospect. Let's review:

- State your understanding of your prospect's problem, opportunity, interest, or concern.
- Describe the firm's ability to deal with those issues in the form of a fact or feature.
- Give to the prospect a benefit that relates to that ability.
- Provide evidence to prove you can deliver what you promise.
- Get confirmation from the prospect that the benefit is important to her.

Before proceeding, let's explore an ingredient that can add excitement and impact to your presentation: showmanship.

SHOWMANSHIP

You definitely need to use showmanship in your selling. Exactly what is showmanship? It is not being a clown or an actor or pulling tricks out of a box like a magician. It *is* a way of making your presentation more interesting, more exciting, more different, and, most important, more effective than your competitors'.

Over the years, showmanship has played an important role in selling ideas and products. For example, few people believed airplanes could really fly until the Wright Brothers flew 852 feet in 59 seconds at Kitty Hawk, proving demonstration to be one of the strongest types of showmanship. Thomas Edison chartered a special train that carried 3000 people to Menlo Park, N.J., to view for themselves an entire town lighted by electricity. J. Walter Thompson coined a new slogan for Woodbury soap: "A Skin You Love to Touch," which introduced sex into advertising, a theme that was to add billions of dollars to the advertising business. Think of Carrie Nation breaking up saloons with her famous hatchet to dramatize her war on "demon rum." There are countless other examples of how lesser-known people using less spectacular methods have been able to help sell their products, services, and ideas. And you can do the same, although at the moment you may be shaking your head and thinking, "Showmanship is fine for those jazzy products, but not for what I'm trying to sell."

Showmanship makes your presentation more effective because it:

- Transfers the prospect's attention from something she may be thinking about or looking at to you or your product
- Connects your service with something of interest to the prospect
- Explains more clearly how your service works
- Presents you and your firm as creative and innovative
- Helps the prospect remember you and your presentation

These are all important benefits, especially when you are trying to make some distinction between you and your competition. There is no limit to the imagination you can use in thinking of novel ideas and approaches, provided that they are *relevant* to what you are talking about, in *good taste* so that nobody is embarrassed, and *comfortable* to use.

In the 1932 World Series against the Chicago Cubs, Babe Ruth electrified the crowd when he dramatically pointed to the centerfield bleachers and then proceeded to hit a home run to exactly that place. By first setting up the confrontation with his gesture and then hitting the ball there, Ruth displayed consummate showmanship!

Do not mistake showmanship for "hotdogging." Babe Ruth's risk-taking heroics (he could have struck out) are quite different from the wild antics of football players who go into weird gyrations when sacking a quarterback or catching a touchdown pass. The professional, whether athlete or salesperson, uses showmanship to enhance the selling objective, not to gloat over success.

Now, let us explore some general approaches to showmanship with a few examples to stir your imagination.

1. Do something unexpected. Most prospects view CPAs as being fairly predictable. With the right prospect you could try something a little different and present another dimension to the stereotyped image. One CPA partner suggests to the prospect that they both bring all the members of their respective teams together at a meeting to exchange questions, ideas, and what is needed to work effectively together. What is unexpected and different is having lower-level people meet before the engagement is sold.

2. Get the prospect involved. This is easier with a tangible product, for example, having the prospect sit down before a computer and try out a software program you are selling. For something less tangible, one CPA asks the prospect to work with him in planning the timing of the audit engagement.

3. Use a striking exhibit. Many accountants and consultants are now using charts and graphs to capture the attention of their prospects, but how about the CPA who has a miniature world map drawn on a golf ball and rolls it toward the prospect saying, "Our worldwide service can help you have your total operation in the palm of your hand." Invariably the prospect chuckles and sometimes asks if he can get one. Even if you don't get the sale, this prospect will have a reminder of your visit.

4. Show a photograph that will interest the prospect. One consultant who deals in management services makes it a habit to show photographs of good and bad examples of plant operations. If he is showing the prospect's own operation, he is sure to be tactful in his presentation so as not to embarrass people he may be working with later.

5. Have the prospect take a quick pencil and paper test that deals with some aspect of her operation. This can help the prospect to see exciting or potential problems without having them pointed out by you, which can hasten agreement that corrective action is needed.

6. Solve a problem of the prospect before you get the engagement. One CPA tries before the meeting to identify one problem of the prospect that she can possibly solve. She presents her solution or approach at the meeting to demonstrate her interest and ability.

7. Demonstrate your product or service. As mentioned, this is one of the most effective tools of showmanship. It is most applicable for demonstrating products, but it can also be used in selling the less tangible services. A few guidelines should be followed if you plan to demonstrate:

- Plan your demonstration in advance. Think of different ways to do it and select the best one. If necessary write out what you want to say, preferably in brief notes.
- Rehearse your demonstration until it becomes smooth. This will avoid your mixing up your words or mishandling your product at the meeting with the prospect. Let an associate or friend see and criticize your rehearsal.
- Let the prospect know that you will be making a demonstration and be sure to arrange for any special equipment you will need, such as projectors, special wiring, etc.
- As you demonstrate, relate the appropriate benefits to the specific needs of your prospect's business.
- Whenever possible, have the prospect participate in the demonstration—handling it, working on a specific problem, anything that will give the prospect greater familiarity and comfort with the product.
- During the demonstration, periodically check to see that the prospect understands what is happening; answer any questions that arise.
- When the demonstration is completed, put the product or material aside, but close enough to refer to if necessary.

This section on showmanship not only should provide you with a few ideas to attempt but it also should stimulate your imagination to think of things you would like to try. Ask salespeople you know for their ideas and techniques. Read sales books that list examples of showmanship. Once you become convinced of its effectiveness, you will make it part of your selling skills.

We have covered in depth the five-part formula for presenting your firm's capability. We have also suggested that you employ, wherever possible in this process, techniques of showmanship. When you have completed this step of the selling process, you might say to the prospect something like, "Ms. Parker, that pretty well sums up what I see as your major interests and how we would help you deal with them. Do you have any questions or is there something else you would like to discuss?" What happens next is covered in Chapter 9.

SKILL-BUILDING TECHNIQUES

Fix firmly in your mind the five-part structure for presenting your firm's capability. Use this structure at least three times in your meeting with the prospect. Complete the following presentation worksheet each time before the meeting. Include examples of showmanship whenever possible.

PRESENTATION WORKSHEET

1. State one problem, need, or opportunity of your prospect.

2. Describe your firm's ability to help (one fact).

3. Show your prospect benefit(s) that relate to that ability.

4. Provide evidence to support your ability to deliver the benefit.

5. Confirm benefits with prospect.

Chapter Nine

Answering the Prospect's Objections

A gratifying response to your last question in Chapter 8 would be, "No, I have no further questions. I'd like to engage you as my accountant." However, realistically, you probably will hear a few tough questions concerning some problems the prospect has with your service, reasons why she cannot retain you, or worse, silence. All these responses or lack thereof are types of objections, and unless you deal effectively with them, there is little chance you will close the sale.

Objections can occur at any time during the selling presentation, but usually you can expect to receive them right after you have made your presentation. The prospect may have problems with something you have said or something you have not said.

In dealing with this important section of your presentation, Chapter 9 discusses the following:

- Why prospects raise objections
- Your attitude toward objections

- Uncovering objections
- Types of objections
- When to answer objections
- A structure for answering objections
- Answers to specific objections

WHY PROSPECTS RAISE OBJECTIONS

The prospect does not raise objections because she doesn't want to buy. She knows that she needs what you or your competitor are offering, whether that need is a compliance audit, sound tax advice, or money-saving management services. As a buyer, she is never absolutely sure that she will be happy with her decision, so she finds reasons not to buy. Sometimes these reasons are sound; sometimes they are excuses for not reaching a decision to buy. All buyers go through this process when they are about to buy a substantial product or service. Think of something of significant value that you have bought for business or personal use. You probably had some doubts about making the purchase, and perhaps you expressed these doubts to the salesperson as confrontational statements, tough questions, or periods of silence. When you are selling your service, expect the same kind of response or behavior from your prospects. In most situations, they are not trying to give you a hard time—they are looking for help in making a decision. What they say or do not say, however, rarely shows that they are looking for help. Here is one CPA's experience:

I had known George for several years and during this period we had discussed from time to time his engaging our services. I had had several opportunities to tell him how he would benefit from our knowledge of his industry and our businessman's approach. He was always agreeable and readily admitted that we had what he needed. When we finally arranged a meeting in his office to nail it down, he suddenly became a different man. I couldn't believe it. That smiling, agreeable, receptive person became a hard-faced tough SOB who raised one reason after another why he shouldn't engage us. It's a good thing I recognized his need to resist, and I hung in there until we reached agreement.

Obviously every prospect is not going to change from a Dr. Jekyll to a Mr. Hyde at some stage in the sale, but buyer resistance is a natural reaction to the buying process. This reaction may become stronger as the prospect realizes he is getting closer to making a decision in your favor. Your ability to overcome this resistance will depend to a large extent on your attitude toward receiving objections.

YOUR ATTITUDE TOWARD OBJECTIONS

If you react to the objection defensively or take it as a personal insult, you will be in trouble. Often, you will have enough of a problem just coming up with a good answer without letting a negative attitude get in your way. Instead, look at the prospect's objections as her way of saying, "Give me more information that will help me reach a decision." So even if you have made an outstanding presentation of what your firm can do for the prospect, prepare yourself to hear objections and welcome them instead of fearing or resenting them.

UNCOVERING OBJECTIONS

You may be thinking, "Well, I can see the need to prepare myself for handling objections, but if none were raised, then I would not have to worry about the problem at all." Wrong. That is when you really have to worry. It's extremely rare for a prospect not to have at least one or two objections. When prospects do not voice objections, it is often because they are reluctant to do so. Sometimes they really do not have any, because, heaven forbid, they are not at all interested in what you have told them, in which case you go back to research, more questions, and a different presentation. Literally, you go back to square one; you have been on the wrong track.

Reluctance to voice the objection is a more likely reason for the prospect's silence. Why would a prospect not voice an objection that is in his mind? It could be one of several things. One may be that he does not want to confront you; he thinks it will result in an unpleasant disagreement. Another is that he thinks voicing an objection will offend you. A third is that he does not like you and does not want to help you. A fourth reason is that he is afraid that you will effectively answer his objection and he will then be that much closer to having to make a decision to buy.

It should be clear that your aim must be to uncover objections that may exist in the prospect's mind. Unless you do, those objections will remain a barrier to completing the sale. You can successfully uncover objections if you project an attitude that is nonthreatening to the prospect and indicates a sincere willingness on your part to hear the objections. Here is one colleague's idea of how to express such an attitude:

Throughout the whole selling process, I try to get across to the prospect my willingness to hear whatever he has to say, good or bad. In fact, right before I present how we can help him, I usually say something like, "Mr. Greene, I believe we've got the kind of service you're looking for, and I'm confident I can demonstrate that, but it's unlikely that you're going to accept or agree with everything I say. So, I hope you'll feel free to tell me when that happens. We've got an important decision to make, and it's essential that we can discuss all aspects involved in that decision."

However, presenting this willingness to discuss objections does not, by itself, always uncover objections. Sometimes, you have to help along the way with simple questions or statements. For example, when completing the five-part module discussed in Chapter 8, the last part was a confirmation statement or question aimed at getting agreement from the prospect on your selling point. Instead of getting agreement, you could get an objection from the prospect. That is not as good as agreement, but at least you know how the prospect feels.

Another way to bring objections to the surface is to ask the prospect what she thinks about something you have just said. Most people like to give their opinions, especially when it concerns them.

Sometimes, you have to be more direct. If a prospect looks uncomfortable, doubtful, or upset while you are talking, you might just stop and say, "Mr. Parker, you look bothered by something I have said. Could you tell me what it is?"

In summary, you want to uncover every objection that concerns the prospect. When you have answered all her objections to her satisfaction, then her mind will be open to reaching agreement.

TYPES OF OBJECTIONS

A prospect can raise innumerable objections. It is impossible to think of every one because every situation has the potential to create one that has never been voiced. However, certain objections are heard pretty often (later, we will list a number of them). Objections can come in the form of a tough question, "How come you guys lost the X engagement?"; a challenging statement, "Your office doesn't have one client in my industry"; or a variety of more subtle responses. In general, objections fall into two categories: those clients consider moderately serious and those they consider very serious. For a moderately serious objection, the prospect may accept a less than fully satisfying answer, but for a very serious objection, only an answer that fully or almost fully satisfies will be acceptable. It is important, albeit difficult, to distinguish between moderately serious and very serious objections so that you can allocate the appropriate amount of time and effort to your response.

Other types of objections have been identified in books on selling. One type is the biased, or prejudiced, objection in which the prospect is speaking more from emotion than logic. Another is the uninformed objection in which the prospect makes a comment for which he has little evidence or support. A third is the delay statement, the meaning of which is self-evident. Although we will discuss the strategies for responding to these types, for the moment it is important that you recognize that objections come in many forms and that you must treat each one as a challenge to overcome.

WHEN TO ANSWER OBJECTIONS

Ideally, objections should be answered at the time the prospect raises them. She is looking for immediate satisfaction, and it makes sense to take care of her objections right away. However, there are exceptions to this rule. For example, there are times when you will wish to answer an objection *before* it is raised. You may question the wisdom of this, saying, "Why create a problem? I've got enough problems just answering the objections that the prospect raises." Perhaps, but the idea is not to *create* objections; it is to state those that you suspect already exist in the prospect's mind. Why do this? You do it to get rid of the objection, since as long as a prospect has an objection, it is a barrier to the sale. Also, as long as she is thinking about that objection, it interferes with her listening carefully to what you say. Finally, the prospect will not defend an objection brought up by you as fiercely as she will defend her own personal objection. All right, how do you identify the specific objections that you should raise before the prospect does? In general, these objections can be identified through your research, through what others have told you about the prospect, or through your experience with similar prospects or clients. When you have heard a particular objection enough times, you can be pretty sure that it is in the mind of your present prospect, and it makes sense to raise it before she does.

When you do raise an objection before the prospect does, try to phrase it so it does not sound like an objection. For example, if you believe your prospect thinks your firm may be too big for him, you may want to say something like, "You know, Mr. Franklin, growing companies like yours sometimes wonder exactly what a larger accounting firm can do for them. I'd like to tell you . . ." A statement like this is relatively nonthreatening and gives you the chance to deal with the subject on your terms rather than being surprised later in the selling process.

There are also times when you will want to *postpone* answering a prospect's objection. One time is when you obviously do not know the right answer and you need time to get the facts. Never guess at answers to objections. State frankly what you do not know, that you will get the answer later, and then make sure that you supply the answer.

Another time you want to postpone your answer is when a long involved answer will interrupt the flow of what you are saying. You can do this tactfully by saying something like, "Mr. Scolari, you've anticipated something I'm going to discuss. If it's all right with you, I'd like to respond to your question in a few minutes." Rarely will a prospect deny you that request if you present it in a tactful way.

Some books on selling say there are times when you *never* answer an objection, for example, when an objection either is unanswerable, e.g., "I'm going into bankruptcy," or is so trivial that it is not worth answering. This approach makes sense if you guard against not giving a valid objection the proper attention because you thought it was trivial. That could upset a prospect.

A STRUCTURE FOR ANSWERING OBJECTIONS

There is no set way for answering objections, but certain principles of human interaction, if put together in a reasonable order, can help you to do the job effectively. One such order follows—try it. When you're comfortable with it, you can experiment and move things around to fit your style. The suggested order is:

1. Stop talking and listen.
2. Clarify if necessary.

3. Probe for deeper meaning.
4. Acknowledge the objection.
5. Answer the real objection.
6. Confirm your answer.

Let's go through these steps one at a time, and then we'll tie them together with an example.

Stop talking and listen.   This seems too obvious to even mention, yet many salespeople are so obtuse and lacking in empathy that they do not know enough to shut up when a prospect raises an objection. No wonder they have difficulty answering an objection, since they never heard it. Listening is more than just hearing. Active listening requires you to nod, look attentive, occasionally grunt or make some audible sound, and generally present a completely responsive appearance to the prospect.

Clarify if necessary.   Sometimes what the prospect is objecting to is very clear, and you can begin your response. Other times the prospect may string together several related or unrelated statements for several minutes, or one objection may be hopelessly disorganized and jumbled. It would be suicide to try to answer objections effectively without first clarifying them. Therefore, you must sort out the multi-objection response by saying, "Ms. Jorden, you mentioned several points that I'd like to respond to. As I recall, first you said . . . , then you said . . . , Have I included all your points?" You can respond to the disorganized or jumbled objection by first saying, "Mr. Ballard, what I think I heard you say was that you . . . . Is that about right?" If you clarify difficult to understand objections before trying to answer them, you will ultimately come up with a better response, probably helping the prospect to see things more clearly in the process.

Probe for deeper meaning.   A prospect may tell you exactly what's bothering her and why she is bothered. More often, though, you will get a superficial objection that doesn't really get to the core of her discomfort. This will require you to do some tactful probing, similar to that discussed in Chapter 7. Now it's even more important for you to uncover the prospect's real problem; if you do not, it could ruin your chances for closing successfully. What you're really looking for are the consequences of the objection, that is, how whatever the prospect is questioning or objecting to affects him. Let's say your prospect says, "I do not want to get involved with a smaller accounting firm." Here are three different questions to use to probe further for the consequences of that statement.

1. "Why does that concern you, Ms. Foster?"
2. "How can that adversely affect you, Mr. Linder?"
3. "What's happened to make you feel that way, Ms. Johnson?"

If the prospect responds honestly to any of these questions, you will be a lot closer to selecting a more satisfying answer. Of course, you may be required to probe a few more times until you have identified the real issue, but it is invariably worth the effort.

Acknowledge the objection. This simply means starting your answers with some statement that acknowledges the importance of the prospect's objections, no matter how insignificant the objection may sound to you. The acknowledgment is really your way of respecting the prospect's right to say what he wants and does not necessarily mean you agree with the objection. In other words, it's a statement that opens a prospect's ears to hear your answer. Here are some examples of this acknowledgment statement:

- "Mr. O'Hare, I can understand your concern about . . . ."
- "Ms. Freidman, that's an interesting point you raised."
- "Mr. Ratner, if I were in your place, I'd probably feel the same way."
- "Ms. Feeley, several other executives have raised that question."

If you have previously used several probing questions, then your acknowledgment statement should be directed to the particular issue you wish to answer, usually the real objection.

Answer the real objection. Now you have the opportunity to respond to your prospect's concern. There are unlimited numbers of objections and unlimited answers, but some general answers will fill many situations. One of the most effective answers is the "boomerang," or "reverse," technique, which turns a prospect's objection into a reason to buy. The very thing she objects to becomes a selling point. Here is how it works:

Prospect
(After a few probes) "I'm afraid you guys are too big for a company my size."

You
"Mr. Buckner, I can understand your concern. We are larger than your present firm. That may be the very reason why you should engage us, because we can provide a growing company like yours with the variety of expertise you require."

In your response you started with an acknowledgment, "Mr. Buckner, I can understand your concern."; then you found something to agree with, but you changed the negative expression "too big" to "we are larger than your present firm." You followed with the boomerang statement: "That may be the very reason you should engage us." Finally, you finished with a benefit to the prospect: "because we can provide a growing company like yours with a variety of expertise." This technique may seem a little complicated, but it can be dramatically effective when used in the right situation.

Another type of answer is used to clarify. In the middle of your conversation, the prospect says, "It's too complicated." What she is really saying is that she does not understand, but that may be too ego-deflating to admit. Therefore your response might be, "Ms. Foster, it is a rather complex system. I'd like to explain it in a little more detail." As you can see, the technique used here is to *explain* something that appears too complicated.

A third type of answer is really a prelude to an answer. It is used when the prospect's objection is clearly true or false. If the objection is a true statement about your service, then you have no other choice than to admit the truth of the statement. However, if the statement is false or clearly inaccurate, you have an equal responsibility to tell that to the prospect. One CPA had this experience:

I remember a situation where one of the other firms in town had a client involved in a fraud. It wasn't a really big deal, but it did make the local papers. For some reason, a prospect I was talking to thought it was our firm that was involved. In a very firm but friendly way, I told him that we were not the firm involved.

In either case, whether you admit or deny the accuracy of a prospect's objection, you should follow up your reply with either additional questions or added benefits, depending on the situation.

Earlier in the chapter, we mentioned the prejudiced, or biased, objection. We said it was not possible to answer that type of objection with logic because the prospect was not in a logical frame of mind. How then do you deal with such an emotionally based objection? Carefully, as this example illustrates:

I was at the Rotary Club and was speaking to a fellow I had met just a few minutes before. When he found out the firm I was with he said, "You guys were my brother's accountant a few years ago. As a result of your advice, he went out of business." He was correct in that we were his brother's accountants, but I knew there were other more serious factors that led to his brother's business failure. My first reaction was to tell him this, but instead, I expressed my regret about his brother's situation and then calmly asked him why he thought we were to blame. As I suspected, he had little evidence to support his accusation and eventually wound up saying that his brother wasn't that good a businessman and probably was chiefly to blame for his own misfortune. No, this person did not become a client, but at least we talk when we see each other.

The prejudiced objection and the uninformed objection are best answered by asking the prospect why she feels the way she does or where she got her information. You may not always succeed in winning these people as clients, but you will have the satisfaction of effectively confronting difficult and sensitive situations.

Confirm your answer.   The last step in answering objections is simply to ask the prospect if she is satisfied with your response to her objection—no big deal, just a question like, "Jane, have I satisfied your concern about that issue?" If she says yes, you can put the objection aside and get on with whatever is next. If she says no or the equivalent, then you have more work to do, but at least you know where you stand on that issue.

When you believe you have answered all your prospect's objections, you're ready to move for the close (see Chapter 10). But first, the following example illustrates the entire process for answering an objection. Then Chapter 9 closes with a list of the more prevalent objections a CPA may hear. To illustrate the entire process for answering an objection, we will simulate a conversation between a prospect and our CPA salesperson. As we go through the dialogue, identify the specific steps we have just covered.

Prospect
"Well, don't get me wrong. I'm pleased that a firm your size would be interested in a small outfit like mine, but you've got lots of big clients to take

care of. Anyhow, not too many accountants really understand the travel industry, and I'm not so sure, considering your fee, whether it's worth it for us to get involved with you. Besides, we've had good service from one guy for over 20 years."

Salesperson

"Jim, you've just voiced several concerns about our chance to work together. I'd like first to see if I heard all these correctly. First, you questioned whether a firm our size would be interested in a business your size; then you raised a doubt as to whether we know enough about the travel industry; you voiced concern about the size of our fee; and finally, you're not sure how to go about changing accountants—if that's something you want to do. Have I got that about right?"

Prospect

"Yeah, not exactly, but close enough."

Salesperson

"Jim, those are all important issues, and if its OK with you, I'd like to deal with them one at a time."

Prospect

"OK, shoot."

Salesperson

"Let's look at your first question, your concern about our relative size. Can you go into that a little more?"

Prospect

"Hell, you're an international firm with all those Fortune 500 clients, offices all over the country, thousands of employees. Why do you need an outfit like mine that's hoping to gross $10 million next year?"

Salesperson

"I'll answer that question in a minute, but you seem to be troubled by the size of some of our larger clients. Why is that?"

Prospect

"Oh, come on, Bill. Their fees are probably at least twenty times more than ours would be. Suppose you get a call from me and a call from them at the same time. Who are you going to take care of?"

Salesperson

"Then what you're really concerned about is that you won't get the attention from us that you're going to need when you need it."

Prospect

"That's about it. Nothing personal, but it's hard for me to see you treating me as a priority."

Salesperson

"OK Jim, I can understand your concern. Some of our clients in businesses your size originally felt the same way. I'd like to tell you our firm's position on this. First of all, we do not view your business as small; you are a growing business with a great deal of potential. We like to be associated with growing businesses. When you do well, we do well. Some of our largest clients were smaller than you when we first started to serve them, and we like to believe we contributed to their growth and success. Here is how we do it. As a growing business, you are not yet in the position to hire all the experts you might like to have. We can provide that expertise for you in areas like tax strategies, financial planning, and systems analysis, just to name a few of the areas in which you've mentioned a need. I can't guarantee that I will be available every time you call, but I will respond as soon as possible. And we certainly will have to be here often enough to learn your operation, become acquainted with your people, and get started on your immediate needs. Does that satisfy your concern about getting the right attention?"

Prospect

"Well, yes. If it's more than just a promise, I'm satisfied."

Salesperson

"It is, Jim. Now, about your question regarding our knowledge of the travel industry. . . ."

The above answer was one way of responding to the specific objection. You may have thought of other ways. That's fine. The purpose of the example was to demonstrate the process, not a pat answer.

APPROACHES TO COMMON OBJECTIONS

Chapter 9 concludes by discussing some of the more common objections. Rather than giving specific answers, we'll present one or more general approaches and let you adapt them to your own needs. Test yourself by working the approach into the process we've just described.

Objection 1.   "Let me think about it awhile."

Some prospects really have a problem making a decision. They are not sure the relationship is going to work out, and the decision to buy a firm's services has greater consequences than buying a new type-writer or a television set. Consider these responses to such procrastination:

When the prospect agrees we're right for him but can't make a decision, I do not push. First I determine if there are any other unanswered objections. If not, then I have a lot of empathy for his need to give careful thought to an important decision. I follow up the meeting with a letter reviewing my understanding of his situation and how I can help him reach his objectives. This gives him something tangible to reflect upon and helps prevent him from conveniently forgetting the need to make a decision.

I arrange for another meeting. I review with him again his major problems and areas of interest and how we can help him. Then I tactfully point out that it's important for him not to delay, and I select certain areas that need immediate attention and show him how we can help him avoid problems, save money, or make money. People will often take action only when a sense of urgency is clearly seen.

With the procrastinator, it's important not to get discouraged after a few "nos." A prospect may be testing my interest, and if I hang in there, the "no" becomes "maybe" and then "yes."

Objection 2.   "You do not have clients in my industry."

The prospect is really trying to tell me I do not understand his business and he thinks I won't be able to give him or his people good advice. He may also be concerned that he's going to have to spend a lot of time educating my engagement team. I usually point out that while I do not have clients who are in the exact same business, I do have clients whose operations and problems are similar, and then I demonstrate how I helped one of my clients who had a similar problem. I practice this technique by reviewing my present clients in diverse industries who share similar problems, areas of interest, and operating strategies. I use them as examples to support my contention that you do not need to have clients in the exact business to do a good job for a prospect.

Another approach I use in answering this objection is to admit I do not have the industry expertise but that we are so anxious to break into that industry that we're willing to spend additional time (at our expense) to learn the business. I tell the prospect he'll be getting an extraordinary effort from people who are motivated by the unique opportunity to get involved in a new industry.

Objection 3. "I'm happy with my present accountant, why change?"

This is the situation that is toughest for me to counter. It is difficult to get someone to change if they are basically happy with their current accountants. I deal with this in two ways. First, I ask them why they like their present accountants. Then I begin to pose specific questions that their present accountants are not raising, and I offer answers to these questions. The idea is not to knock their present firm but to raise their expectations of their accountants.

I tell them they should not have all their eggs in one basket, that it makes sense for them to have another source of expertise available in case they become dissatisfied with their present firm some time in the future. I then ask for an opportunity to do a small job so I can demonstrate my ability.

Objection 4. "How can I let my present accountant go after 20 loyal years?"

I remember one prospect that was reluctant to come with us because he didn't know what to do with his present accountant who had been doing the job for almost 20 years. The prospect recognized his need for more sophisticated help but felt a sense of loyalty to his old accountant plus a good dose of potential guilt if he let him go. We were able to work out an arrangement where his old accountant retained a portion of the work and we picked up the more advanced work. Surprisingly, it's worked out very well for everyone and, eventually, we may wind up with the whole engagement.

This is an emotionally charged objection, and I know I must handle it tactfully, but I'm not afraid to confront the prospect. I acknowledge and show respect for the close feeling he has with his long-time accountant, but I also let him know he has a commitment to his growing business, and if that business is to continue to grow it must get the best possible help. I usually finish by telling him that tough business decisions and good feelings do not always go together.

Objection 5. "How do I know the rest of your team is as good as you?"

The question or objection I hear most is the one about the quality of the people who will be working on the engagement. Nobody's ever questioned the quality of our firm, but the prospect doesn't deal with the "big firm in the sky"; he deals with three or four people, and he wants to make sure they know what they're doing. So, I make sure he meets the manager and senior at one of our first meetings. I want him to see they have something to say about his business so he can assess their interest and knowledge.

Objection 6.   "I used to be with a CPA firm so don't try to snow
                me."

The toughest objection for me is justifying the amount of work we need to do to a controller or vice president of finance who previously was in public accounting; sometimes they even worked for us. He knows there are a lot of audit steps that merely give us some assurance that everything is OK. He can appreciate the need to do these steps, but he also feels an obligation, in his corporate position, to get the most value from the audit. I usually appeal to his professionalism, using his background as a CPA, to weigh the amount of work against the risks of underauditing. If he's retained his so-called conservative training, he may bitch a little but he'll ultimately agree. If he's turned into a "bottom-line watchdog," then we have a problem, and I try to determine how we can help him achieve his individual goals.

Objection 7.   "I don't know much about accounting and I sure don't
                know what I'm getting for my money."

It's tough to justify the amount of work we do to corporate executives who do not have much of a financial background. They're used to see-ing a direct payoff for effort expended, and it's hard for them to grasp the concept of work done to avoid a potential risk or to give assurance that everything is OK. I'll usually try to sell the idea on the basis that, because of the work we do, we'll be able to offer some worthwhile business suggestions in our management letter. If that doesn't sell, I remind them that if we do not satisfy ourselves as to the healthy con-dition of their business, we may have to issue a qualified report. I hate to resort to that because it's a real negative alternative.

Objection 8.   "I'm a small business and do not need all that sophis-
                ticated help."

The prospect in a small business may say he is concerned with the fee, but that's tied in with his thinking he's going to get a lot of sophis-ticated work from us that he really doesn't need. I usually can over-come that by pointing out that his needs are different from those of a larger company and that we have no intention of twisting his needs to fit a larger client-audit program. That would be as unproductive for us as it would be for him. Instead, I try to identify a specific problem he is wrestling with and give him some free advice on how to deal with it. Then I tell him that's an example of the kind of service he can expect.

Objection 9.   "My banker wants me to stay with my present firm."

I'm glad when a banker supports our firm this way with one of our clients, but it really doesn't hold water. To counter, I mention the name of another banker I know at his branch, or say I have a number of contacts at other banks who would be very eager for his business. I might even suggest these bankers call him. Even if it doesn't work out, at least I've tried to help these bankers, and they may very well reciprocate.

Objection 10.   "We're concerned that one of our major competitors is a client of yours."

This objection is the opposite of the one that says we do not know enough about their industry. You're damned if you do and damned if you don't. I counter this by pointing out that we'll have different people on both engagements and that they'll get the benefit of industry expertise without the concern of loss of confidentiality. If they persist, I firmly tell them that we're a professional firm and would be damn fools to risk our reputation by violating any confidence of our clients.

Objection 11.   "Your fee is too high."

Paying our fee can be a big stumbling block for a company that's used to paying less to a smaller accounting firm. I try to overcome this resistance by showing them an immediate saving. For example, I'll ask to review their last 3 years' tax returns. Often we can come up with a tax refund that will exceed our first-year fee. I'd estimate we're able to do that on more than half the new business we bring in.

Sometimes you have to negotiate certain aspects of the fee with the prospect. For example, about 6 months ago, I was talking with a prospect in a proposal situation. Our fees were higher than our competition in tax work, audit, and training their new bookkeepers. After discussing it, they said they could live with the tax and training fees but thought the audit fee was out of line. I told them for the first year we would match the quote they got from the other firm for the audit part of the engagement. That did it, and now they're a satisfied client.

If I think the fee is a real problem in their minds, I'm going to deal with it up front. I do not want them thinking about that problem instead of listening to what we've got to say. Depending on what they say, I may say, "Initially, we're going to put in a lot of work for which we are not going to charge you. We consider our learning curve to be an investment in you." This is a good argument when we're not as strong in a particular industry as we'd like to be and need the time to learn.

The more sophisticated buyer in a larger organization isn't really objecting to the fee. He's probably used to paying big fees and also charging big fees for his own business. What he wants is meaningful service for that fee. I remember a discussion with the general manager of a major corporation. He said, "I do not mind paying your fee but I expect you to find things my people do not find or explain things I do not understand." Apparently, he was not getting that from his present accountants.

Sometimes a prospect will object to a fee but not really mean it. He just doesn't want to give in too easily. If I think it's not a really big objection, I'll just acknowledge his statement, but I won't try to defend or negotiate the fee. Of course, I have to be careful not to offend him by giving him the idea that I'm deliberately ignoring his objection.

Justifying a professional fee can be tough at times, particularly in our business where the client doesn't know exactly what we do or care how we do it. If I know who his attorney is, I have a pretty good idea what he's paying in legal fees, and if it's about the same fee basis as ours, I'll compare our contribution to that of his attorneys. Then he recognizes that he's already paying a first-class professional fee and he's apt to be more agreeable to our fee.

I tell him his business is on the way up and deserves the best kind of service and that that kind of service costs more than what he's been paying. Of course, that's a pretty aggressive approach, but I'm careful to use it only to the kind of people who like to be spoken to in that way.

For government jobs, often the contract goes to the low bidder, almost never to the high bidder. The idea is to get some idea of how much the competitive bids are so you can position your bid in the right range. That's why it's so important to have a network of contacts. Also, the acceptable fee is usually subject to the thinking and influence of the current administration. If the administration cuts government spending, this will obviously affect the amount of work available and, consequently, the fee to get this work.

Some people have read the financial report put out by some of the accounting firms and have seen the average partner salaries. They put two and two together and figure out that a large part of the fee is going into partner income. If their own business has a relatively low profit margin, they could object to our margin. I counter this argument by mentioning the risk, knowledge, and work involved in giving an opinion on a company's financial condition. I quote a few examples. I suspect that with the exposure the profession is getting, there will be more clients raising this point.

In many cases, it's a matter of education. The prospect just doesn't understand what the fee is paying for and why that work is important to him. If you can get him to listen, you may have a chance to explain some of the facets of the audit, but you'd better pick things he can understand and relate to. For example, clients with a large number of customers can understand the need for what we do on receivables and bad-debt reserves. A client with a large inventory can appreciate the importance of what we do in counting and evaluating that inventory. But, I won't try to explain some of the more technical steps we do.

If a person objects to a high fee, sometimes I'll quietly ask him why he thinks it's high. At that point, he's liable to say anything or practically nothing. At least I have something to answer to. Often it's just a feeling he has about the fee, and it's important to let him express his feelings. Then we can discuss it.

If his business makes or provides a product or service that is of higher quality than his competition and consequently costs more, I describe our service in the same way. He then will have a better appreciation as to why our service may cost more than our competition's.

I'm beginning to see audit committee members raising questions about the fee, not only when we're trying to get new business, but when we're trying to retain our own clients. Some audit committee members are anxious to prove their value to the board of directors or stockholders, and if they're not familiar enough with the business to ask technical questions, then they question the audit fee. Often they have connections on other boards or are trying to push a particular accounting firm and will raise the possibility of getting lower fees for the same amount of work from another firm. It's very tough to defend a fee you've built up over 20 years when your competition is willing to do it for 40 percent less, and it's tougher to justify your willingness to match the lower fee. Of course, everyone knows it is a foot-in-the-door technique and that the fee will go up quickly in subsequent years. But, when a big company is on a cost-cutting drive, a hundred thousand bucks means something. I realize this is more a problem of client re-

tention than bringing in new business, but I think it's a serious prob-
lem, and frankly, I do not have the answer.

To close our discussion of the subject of objections and how to answer them, let's review what you need to know and do.

Understand why prospects raise objections to the engagement and to your services. It is natural to resist change and spending more money or to be cautious about entering into a professional relationship. Become a student of human behavior and you will have a much better understanding of the reason for objections and how to answer them.

Have a healthy attitute toward objections. Do not take objections as a personal affront! They are merely the prospect's way of making sure of a good decision or of delaying one. You may never learn to love objections, but you'll learn to appreciate the need to hear them.

Uncover all objections. As long as the objection does not surface, it remains in the prospect's head as a possible barrier to eventually closing the sale.

Become familiar with the major types of objections. They repeat themselves, and you can almost anticipate many of the ones you hear. Keep in mind that some objections are more serious than others, and those are the ones you should be prepared to answer.

There are different times to answer objections. Usually you will want to answer them at the time they are raised, but sometimes you will want to delay your answer until a more opportune time.

Learn the steps for answering objections. Stop talking and listen. Clarify if necessary. Probe for deeper meaning. Before answering, acknowledge the prospect's right to raise objections; then select the right answer and remember to confirm your answer to make sure the prospect is satisfied.

Finally, practice answering objections. The more you practice the better you get. The better you get, the more sales you close.

SKILL-BUILDING TECHNIQUES

Anticipate at least *five* objections you may receive from your prospect at your next meeting. Using the following worksheet, prepare a response for each one. (At your meeting, for *any* objection received, remember to *first* listen carefully and probe for deeper meaning.)

ANSWERING OBJECTION WORKSHEET

1. State the objection

2. Acknowledge the objection

3. Answer the objection

4. Confirm the answer

Chapter Ten
Reaching Agreement

If you have correctly followed the steps in the previous chapters, there's a good chance you can close the sale or, as we professionals say, reach agreement with the prospect. If you bungled any of the previous steps, do not count on saying some magic closing words that will change disaster into victory. There are none.

When you have reached the closing stage, the prospect has decided in his mind either to buy or not to buy. If he has decided not to buy, that's it. It means going back to a previous step or saying goodbye and trying another day. If you have done a thorough job in the previous steps, then the close becomes a formality to confirm his decision.

Nonetheless, over the years, incalculable numbers of salespeople have turned this formality into a lost sale or, to use a familiar cliché, snatched disaster from the jaws of victory. Why? Here are the basic reasons, and they are as applicable to CPAs as they are to bankers, engineers, and those who sell products.

1. They didn't know when to close.
2. They didn't know how to close.
3. They didn't try to close.

WHEN TO CLOSE—BUYING SIGNALS

Many salespeople, CPAs included, are puzzled about when is the right time to close. Do you close after all objections have been answered, when you can't think of any more benefits, or after a certain number of hours or visits with the prospect? The answer is yes and no, which furthers the confusion. All these answers can be correct, provided that one element is present, an element that cannot be absolutely planned or predicted by you. *The time to close is when the prospect is ready to buy,* and that can happen anytime during the presentation. One colleague interviewed looks for certain signals when deciding when to close:

I used to be very nervous about deciding when to close. I'd sit with a prospect and worry about closing too late and missing the sale or closing too soon and risking being turned down. So a lot of the time, I didn't do either, and that was worse. Later, I began to notice certain words or mannerisms that the prospect would say or make that indicated he was thinking pretty favorably about engaging me.

In selling, these words or mannerisms from a prospect are called *buying signals,* and they tell you that she is ready to buy. It's up to you to recognize these signals. And don't count on obvious signals such as the prospect saying, "OK, I want you to be my accountant." That is not a signal. It is a gift. Because the prospect is probably nervous about getting close to making a decision, her signal is likely to be subtle or even disguised. As we said, the buying signal can be something the prospect says or does. Let us first examine what some CPAs have heard that indicates that the prospect is beginning to see them as their accountant, adviser, or consultant.

They begin to ask questions about which personnel I'm going to put on the job. I remember holding our initial meeting with a prospect, and I had brought a senior accountant with me who really impressed the prospect. At a subsequent meeting, the prospect asked if that person would be on the job. Shortly afterward, we got the engagement.

They probe for an in-depth opinion about a particular problem they may be wrestling with. I'm not talking about the preliminary discussions we have at the initial meeting, when we're trying to identify their main problems and interests. I mean the one problem that may be keeping them up at night and they need good answers. I see this as a test of our knowledge and ability and if we give them some satisfaction, I think we've got the job.

When they start bad-mouthing their present accountants, then I know we've got a real chance. At the beginning, even if they're unhappy with their accountants, they're probably not going to say anything bad about them and that's understandable. In order to get them to the point of actively criticizing their present accountants, you have to do two things. First, probe for exactly what it is that they're unhappy about—lack of expertise, not enough attention, poor personnel on the engagement. Second, you have to establish yourself as a viable and desirable alternative. This means you have to provide everything they're presently not receiving and you have to establish a feeling of trust and confidence so they don't feel uncomfortable about criticizing their present accountants. You're certainly not going to accomplish this in an initial meeting, but it can happen after two or three meetings.

They ask how we would expect the fee to be paid, for example, whether it could be paid in installments. This tells me that he doesn't have a problem with the size of our fee but he might have a cash flow problem. If we can settle that to his satisfaction, he's probably going to take us on. Frankly, it took me a long time to realize that the question about how payment of fee was to be made was a favorable question and was really a buying sign.

They ask about the timing of the audit, when we would send in our team, or when they could expect a statement. This is only another question that they want answered, but sometimes, if the rest of the discussion has been positive, I'll read this question as the last remaining obstacle, and I'll try to reach agreement after answering it.

When I hear a prospect say, "I hadn't really planned to pay that much of a fee," or, "I didn't really think I needed that kind of service," I see a wavering of his resolution and a real signal that he's changing his mind toward us. I'll capitalize on those doubts and try to close the deal. The important thing is to stop selling.

They'll ask if Joe or Bill would be the senior or manager on the engagement or if I would be the partner. They're telling me that they like the people they've met and probably want to work with them. You have to listen for them to use that word "would." To me, it's their *way of preparing themselves to reach agreement with us without appearing to give in to us.*

I remember having a discussion with a prospect who has a medium-sized automobile accessories company. In the middle of our conversation, he suddenly starts telling me what he'd want us to do if we were his accountants. I just shut up and listened, and when he was finished, I said, "OK, we'll do that," and that clinched it. That only happened to me once, but now I sure look out for a prospect to act that way. That was one of the easiest closes I remember.

I've been in a few situations where after the meeting has gone on for a while, one of the prospects makes a favorable comment about our understanding of his business or his problems or how we approach the audit. That's great to hear, but it's important to act on those comments and not just sit there and wait for him to do or say something more.

Those are some of the buying signals you may hear from prospects that indicate they're ready to reach agreement with you. As we previously said, a prospect may also give nonverbal signals that indicate the same readiness to be closed. One CPA gave the following example:

I watch for their body language. They become more relaxed, less tense. There's a lowering of the defensive posture, such as uncrossing their arms or leaning toward me. Their face and voice tone become more friendly. I learned about this in a sales course I took and then read a few books on the subject. It's not a gimmick. It's really helped me to know when a prospect is beginning to warm up.

If you're selling to more than one person at one time it's important to be aware not only of their reactions to you but also of physical signs they give each other. Watching the interaction between two prospects helped the CPA in this example:

I remember talking to two brothers about the possibility of doing some tax work for them. At one point I mentioned the need to set aside funds for their children's education. I must have hit a hot button, because they immediately looked at each other and both nodded almost imperceptibly. I pursued that issue which was the last subject we talked about before reaching agreement.

So, a buying signal can be verbal or nonverbal. However, take care when reading nonverbal signals or, as it is popularly called, "body language." Not every body motion or expression automatically means what you think or want it to mean. For example, when a prospect scratches his head, it could signify deep thought about making a buying decision. Or it could mean he has an itch. Therefore, it is better to look for more than one signal. If you get a cluster of signals that have similar meaning, then you can be more sure of the message you are getting.

If you are lucky, the prospect will give you a very clear buying signal that will encourage you to try to close or reach agreement. Specific closing techniques will be discussed later in this chapter.

THE TRIAL CLOSE

What happens if the prospect's signals are so subtle or unclear that you are not sure whether he is ready to buy or not? Do not despair. You have at your disposal a very effective tool called the *trial close* that has been developed for this very problem.

The purpose of the trial close is to help you find out how close the prospect is to buying, how warm she feels toward your services or product. The trial close is usually posed as a question. It differs from the regular close in that the regular close asks for a *decision*, while the trial close asks for an *opinion*. Thus, you can see that a trial close is much less threatening to both the buyer and the seller.

For example, a "closing" question might be, "How soon can we begin working with you?" while a "trial close" question would be, "How do you feel about working with a firm like ours?" The word "feel" is the key to making this question a trial close. It enables the prospect to express her feelings or opinion without being committed to a decision.

Other examples of a trial close are: "What do you *think* about our approach to your systems problems?"; "*If you were* to engage us, when would you want to start?"; "*Have I demonstrated* our tax expertise to your satisfaction?" With a little thought, you can probably think of a few other phrases that will work as trial closes.

In general, trial closes are most effective after you've had a chance to present the firm's services (Chapter 8) or right after answering a few objections (Chapter 9). However, you can use trial closes earlier in your selling if you sense the prospect is leaning toward engaging you. Note that a trial close differs from the confirmation part of the presentation step (Chapter 8) in that the confirmation asks the prospect's opinion about one specific benefit while the trial close asks the prospect's opinion about agreeing to the engagement.

What are the possible responses to your trial close? The prospect will give one of three basic responses. One, she may give you a negative response, such as, "No, I don't really think you're for us," or "You haven't shown me anything I'm not already getting from my present accountant." If you get this type of response, you've probably been on the wrong selling track all along. You either didn't cover her real needs or you didn't present what you could do for her very well. It could be the end of the sale or, at least, back to the drawing board—more research and questions.

Don't get nervous. The clearly negative response to a trial close is rare. It usually occurs only when you haven't prepared adequately. More often, the prospect, in reply to a trial close, will give you a qualified positive response, followed by questions or objections. For example, if you say, "Ann, does our approach sound like it will help you accomplish your business objectives?", she may say, "Yes, I like your approach, but . . . ." This is a normal and expected response to a trial close. It lets you zero in on answering her specific objections; this, as you learned from Chapter 9, is extremely important if you are to eventually reach agreement. You will have a clearer idea how close the prospect is to engaging you.

The third possible response to your trial close will be a positive one; either the prospect will say, "Yes, I think your approach will help us," or he will nod his head affirmatively and give other positive body signals. When you get that response, you go for the close.

HOW TO CLOSE

In selling accounting services, a close takes place when a prospect agrees to let you begin to do something for her or him. Therefore, it's imperative that some action take place as a result of the close. Your closing statement is designed to let the prospect know its important that you begin working now and also that you're ready to begin. Everything about you should project that feeling of eagerness to begin to work together. To project that feeling, one CPA uses this technique:

When I sense they're close to making a decision in our favor, I raise
my enthusiasm a few notches higher and tell them how excited we are
to begin working with them. Some CPAs have difficulty saying some-

thing like this. I hope all my competition feels that way, because being
able to express my excitement really gives me an edge.

It is important to understand that at the point of close a prospect
may be at her most uncomfortable. Since having to make a decision
may be causing the discomfort, you must help the prospect get
through this. Here is how one CPA interviewed does it:

Sometimes it's tough for a person to make a decision. I'm that way
myself when I've got a big purchase to make. So that person needs a
little understanding or help. For example, if a prospect has been
agonizing over changing accountants for a few months, I'll acknowl-
edge this and say something like, "Joe, I know this is an important
decision for you but you've been worrying about making a change for
2 months now. Why don't you just decide one way or the other so you
can stop worrying about it." Am I taking a risk on his deciding
against us? Sure, but I haven't lost anything, and I've demonstrated a
hell of a lot of understanding for his position and way of thinking.

Often, the prospect may be impressed with one of your people
because of a particular skill or personal quality that person possesses.
In that case you can move the sale to a close by saying something like,
"I know you respect Frank's knowledge of your industry, and I agree
he should be working on your engagement. So I've arranged his
schedule so he can be the manager on your job. In fact, he's ready to
begin next Monday."

Setting specific dates and times is important in moving a prospect
toward a decision. This can be done in a variety of ways with the
intent to make something happen, as this example shows:

I'll suggest that we begin our preliminary work on next Monday or
Tuesday. Or, if I'm not absolutely sure how they feel, I might phrase
it, "Is there any reason why we can't start our work on Monday?" If
there are any remaining objections, that should smoke them out.

Some CPAs have found it effective to establish a sense of urgency
with the prospect, saying in effect that they could be hurt if they do
not make a decision now. This requires putting pressure on the prospect, using phrasing that makes it seem in the prospect's best interest to make a decision.

If we've identified a critical area in his operation, I'll make a comment
to the effect that he really can't afford to neglect that much longer
and that we should get started working on it right away. Would I say
that in writing? Absolutely.

Sometimes a prospect is not really happy with her present accountant but is not ready to make a complete change. Then you go for a piece of the pie, like this accountant did:

I remember one conversation with _____ that went something like this. "Look, I know you've got a few problems with your present accountants but you're really not sure you want to make a change at this point. I can understand that. Why don't you let us look into that tax problem we've been discussing so you can see what we can do for you?" He agreed and was pleased with our findings. We still don't have the audit, but I'm hopeful.

Is submitting a written proposal or letter of engagement before closing the sale necessary? Usually yes, if for no other reason than to get a mutual understanding of the fee or other important terms. If you do submit a proposal or letter, don't count on it as being the vehicle that closes the sale. It's still up to you to make something happen at a particular time. One CPA interviewed acknowledged that responsibility:

Often, of course, we're required to submit some kind of written proposal to them, nothing elaborate but something that states our mutual understanding of what they need, what we can do, and how much it will cost. It is our job to call a couple of days after the delivery of the proposal and find out if there are any remaining questions or problems. If not, I'll suggest that we get started.

Some CPAs have found it more effective to submit the letter of engagement after they've closed. Here's how it's done:

When I'm in a meeting with a prospect, I don't try to sell him any particular service. I spend my time probing for his most critical problems. Once we agree what it is, I say, "OK, let's get started fixing it right now. I'll send you an engagement letter with the fee included." Sure it works. He's so involved with solving his problem, he doesn't give much thought to the formality of closing. Of course, I have a pretty good idea what fee will be acceptable to him, but the whole idea is to get started doing something for him.

That is the real key for closing the sale: getting started on some specific piece of work before you leave the prospect's office. It is important to focus his attention on the solution to some problem that was previously discussed. If you are going to be really assertive about this closing step, you can do the following:

*I try to close the sale by beginning the engagement before the prospect
agrees to it. I do this by getting my hands on something that belongs
to him. I recall talking to a prospect about doing some tax work for
them. I suggested I review their returns for the last 5 years. He
agreed, and I said, "OK, let me have them." He said, "Right now?" I
said, "Of course." He gave them to me and I spent the balance of the
afternoon in his conference room reviewing those returns. There was
never another word about reaching agreement. When he handed over
those returns, the sale was made.*

Some CPAs may consider that approach to be overly aggressive,
but it works. Obviously, such an approach is not right for everyone;
each of us must find the words and actions with which we are comfortable. Nevertheless, even when we recognize the time to close and
we know the right words to use, we sometimes hold back from doing
what needs to be done—*trying* to close.

TRY TO CLOSE

If you've done everything right so far, you have a good chance to
close. But you must first try, especially now that you have the tools to
work with. Closing a sale is a new experience for many of us, and it
can fail. The combination of something new and the potential for
failure provides a potent reason for not trying. Who wants to fail,
look bad, or be rejected by someone? These are understandable reasons for not trying. But you must overcome this fear and turn your
attitude into one that approaches the close with confidence, as did the
CPA who told this story:

*I was the best 95 percent salesman you'll ever see. For 95 percent of
that meeting I was perceptive, knowledgeable, and articulate. My
benefits were on target and made an impact on the prospect. I handled
objections smoothly and confidently. And then, with victory in my
grasp, I would suddenly stop and wait for something to happen. And
nothing would happen. I was waiting for the prospect to close, and he
was waiting for me to close. Now, I know it's my responsibility to try
to close. Sure, I get turned down sometimes, but I win more than I
lose and that's a lot better than nothing happening and wondering
why.*

Trying to close is not unlike the effort made by professional athletes. If a baseball player doesn't swing his bat, he has no way of

getting a hit. The same principle operates for a quarterback who never throws the football or a golfer who doesn't take a full swing when driving off the tee. A successful hit, accurate throw, or well-placed shot first requires the willingness to try, knowing full well that *you will not always succeed.* A baseball player who gets three hits in ten times at bat is acknowledged to be successful, as is the basketball player whose shooting percentage is over 50 percent. So it is in selling. You do not have to close every sale to be successful, but you do have to try to close when the opportunity exists. Otherwise you bat *zero.* Batting zero is not what this book is about, so here are some guidelines for getting you to take a full swing and raising your closing percentage:

1. *Do your homework.* Solid research and preparation give a powerful shot of confidence.
2. *Think positively.* Concentrate on your previous successes. Relive those experiences in your mind. What you did before, you can do again.
3. *Prime yourself.* Before you walk into the prospect's office, give yourself a mental pep talk or, if nobody's around, an audible one. Tell yourself how good you are, what your firm can do, how the prospect is going to do better because of you. Don't laugh at the pep talk idea. Professional entertainers, athletes, and salespeople do it all the time. It's called "getting psyched" for the big moment (see Chapter 11 for more details).
4. *Be prepared to close.* Throughout the sale, remind yourself that you will try to close if the opportunity exists.
5. *Go for it.* Keep looking for buying signals. When you get that intuitive feeling, don't wait for 100 percent assurance. Close!

That's it. You now have gone through the entire selling process. You start with the need to make contact with the prospect to demonstrate your interest and ability for the purpose of setting up another meeting. Then you prepare for that meeting by thorough research, using the 4-P formula. You plan ways to open the meeting on a favorable note, proceeding then to confirming the prospect's needs through effective questioning and careful listening. Based on that input, and using the five-step structure, you present your firm's services in terms of benefits to the prospect, successfully answering tough objections. Finally, through the use of trial closes or recognition of buying signals, you find a way to close the sale by making something happen.

SKILL-BUILDING TECHNIQUES

At your next meeting, keep alert for the prospect to give you subtle buying signals. These will usually occur after you present your firm's capabilities or answer some of the prospect's objections. When you receive the signal, use a trial close. If the response is favorable, try to close the sale by getting agreement to begin some part of the engagement at a specific time, preferably right away.

Chapter Eleven
Cross-Selling Your Services

Until now the material has dealt with selling services to *new* clients almost exclusively. The thought has probably occurred to you that you could use the principles and techniques discussed to expand your business with *existing* clients. Absolutely! Despite the emphasis of this book on bringing in new clients, the fact remains that most additional business comes from existing clients.

Before discussing how to identify and sell additional business, let's discuss for a moment the question of independence, or to put it another way, does an accounting firm have a conflict of interest if it provides additional services to an audit client? This issue has been debated by regulatory and professional groups for years without decisive results. However, all the large firms and most of the smaller ones clearly are providing multiple services, so the question really is how to determine which services a firm feels comfortable with and capable of providing.

James Mahon, in his book, *The Marketing of Professional Accounting*

Services, puts forth a good argument in support of cross-selling your services:

> . . . the conceptual differences between auditing and the consulting services are probably not as wide as they may seem. Audit objectivity and independence are not necessarily weakened by tax consulting for example. There does not seem to be any reason why an accountant of integrity cannot push for a favorable construction of an ambiguous tax regulation while representing his client in government proceedings and, at the same time, insist upon a higher, more conservative provision for the disputed tax in the client's financial statements. . . .
>
> Nor do management consulting services present any substantially different implications. The technical affinity has always been present here, too, as has the commonality of the subject matter. Indeed, management services expertise should enable accountants to better report on the operational aspects of the business and institutions they audit—a practice that would not only serve the growing information needs of mounting absentee owners, but would also add to the productivity and profitability of the organizations themselves. Unfortunately, the profession has just scratched the surface of using consultants' help in auditing.[1]

OPPORTUNITIES FOR OTHER SERVICES

Aside from the so-called ethical issues, what also gets in the way of providing additional services is the sometimes cool relationship that exists between auditors and consultants within the same firm. However, let's discuss this more later in the chapter. First, let's look at the various types of services that a firm can provide to their clients. The following is certainly not a complete list nor are the words necessarily the ones you would use.

- Cash management
- Electronic data processing (EDP) systems and development
- Financial planning and modeling

---

[1]James J. Mahon, *The Marketing of Professional Accounting Services,* John Wiley and Sons, Inc., New York, 1978, pp. 66-67.

- Financial statement analysis
- Individual tax planning
- Mergers and acquisitions
- Cost studies (various)
- Profitability studies
- Employee benefits
- Training programs
- Organizational development
- Feasibility studies (various)
- Pension and profit-sharing plans
- Compensation options
- International operations
- Inventory control and planning
- Accounting methods
- Banking relationships
- Investment opportunities
- Return on investment (ROI) analysis
- Executive search
- Plant expansion

Your client may need one or more of these services. Who is going to provide it? The logical answer is you—you know the client, his plans; his likes and dislikes; his operations, performance, and results. And your client knows you, your knowledge, your experience, how you work, and most important, what you have done for him in the past. Thus it would seem you have the inside track and should get the additional business. Unfortunately, for the incumbent, it doesn't always work out that way. Consider the experience of this client:

We have had the same auditing firm for the last few years. They had done a satisfactory job, not great, but good enough to retain the audit. During a review of our organization it became clear to us that we needed to combine our EDP operations. It also became clear that we would need the help of outside consultants to determine the options available to us and the best possible approach to take. We decided to take bids from a few firms, including our accounting firm. Interestingly, in the course of their audit they had not recommended the need for such a study. Well, in short, we gave the study to another firm. This firm, in addition to coming in with a substantially lower fee (which was not the real issue), spent a lot more time in initially speaking with our people and trying to really get to know our operation. And they delivered a proposal that showed some careful thought. Contrast that with the proposal we received from our accounting firm,

which was twice as long and looked like it had come right off the shelf.
We were quite surprised with their apparent lack of creativity consid-
ering how long they have been working with us.

Call it lack of creativity, inability, or just not caring, this is a case where the firm with the inside track blew it, and in the course of doing so, probably lost some credibility with its client. You cannot take your client for granted, assuming that you will automatically get the additional work. You must sell your client every day as if she were a new prospect. Otherwise, you not only will *not* get more business, you may eventually lose the client.

What do you need to do to successfully cross-sell your services to your clients? Selling to your client follows the same principles and techniques as selling to a prospect. You may not have to worry about making an initial contact, but you still must probe for opportunities and problems, show your interest and expertise, present your service as real benefits to the client, overcome tough questions and objections, and close the sale.

IDENTIFYING CROSS-SELLING OPPORTUNITIES

Where do you begin to look for these opportunities? The obvious place is at the audit. You or your engagement team should conduct the audit not only from a compliance viewpoint but also from the client's business viewpoint. The client rarely gets excited when you tell her that internal control is in good condition, but point out a serious operational problem or an opportunity for additional profit and watch her eyes light up. To do this you will have to look at the business consequences of each audit operation as well as the audit consequences. Or, you may look at the client organization as if you were conducting an operational or management audit. If this sounds foreign to you, don't get stuck in your public accounting ivory tower. Talk to some of the more successful internal auditors; they get paid for being the eyes and ears of management and could probably fill in some of the gaps you have. Also, speak to the client employees. Listen to their ideas and their woes. They work there every day and know the underlying problems that are not easily seen. This is a good time to use your listening and questioning skills. Probe tactfully and confirm what you hear with others.

When you have identified what you perceive to be a problem or opportunity for which you can provide a service, talk to your associates in tax, management services, or whatever. Discuss your thoughts and findings with them to determine if your observations are valid or if they see an opportunity to work with you. Auditors are sometimes reluctant to bring their consultant associates into their engagement, fearing that the new service will not succeed and will therefore upset the client relationship that they have built over the years. This is an organizational problem, not a selling one, and if it is prevalent in the firm, it needs immediate attention.

If a legitimate problem or opportunity exists, try to determine, before rushing in to offer your services, if there is anyone in the client organization that could handle it with or without your help. This may sound like the antithesis of what this book is about, but your first obligation to your client is to give sound advice without necessarily costing more money. And, if you can enhance the career of one of the client personnel you will gain a valuable ally or a power of influence who can support you at a future critical time. At any rate, the client will see you as someone who puts his interests before your own.

SELECTING YOUR ASSOCIATES

If you do determine that your firm can provide the right services for a legitimate client problem or opportunity, decide which of your associates is best equipped to work on the assignment. Certainly the most important ingredient is that person's competence to do the job. Specifically, this includes previous experience with the job to be done, knowledge of the particular industry, and skill at identifying and solving problems. Don't forget the ability to practice good human relations with your client's people. Sometimes this can be a problem, as illustrated by this colleague's story:

I should have known from the beginning that _____ was the wrong person for the job. But I was swayed by his experience in the industry and the particular knowledge he brought to the job. He got along fine with top management, but when he got out on the factory floor, he changed to either a threatening ogre or a condescending phoney. Half-way through, we had to pull him off the job. Thank heavens we were able to replace him with someone to the client's and our satisfaction. With counseling _____ has made improvement in handling people, but his next promotion is a question mark.

APPROACHING THE CLIENT

With the problem or opportunity identified and your associates selected, you are ready to approach the client. This can be done in several ways. One way is to introduce your findings and recommendations in your management letter. This is a bit formal, however, and does not seem to be the best way to ask the client to spend more money. A better way would be to bring up the subject at the conclusion of the audit or at another opportunity for a meeting. If the circumstances are right, you may want to discuss it at lunch. Depending on your client's knowledge of the situation and acknowledgement of the problem or opportunity, you might want to bring your associates to the meeting. You may also, if it is to your advantage, suggest that a person from the client's organization attend (again, the power of influence). At the appropriate time you should introduce the subject by getting your client's attention with one of the methods discussed in Chapter 6. Briefly and clearly, outline the essence of the situation and particularly its *consequence* to her or her organization. Wait for her reaction. If she has not already done so, get her to acknowledge your appraisal of the situation. Encourage your client to ask questions and even challenge your position. You cannot introduce a solution or approach until your client has indicated some agreement that she sees the situation the same way you do.

Once you get some acknowledgement that the client agrees with your analysis of the situation, proceed with what you think needs to be done. It is important that you or your associates suggest *more than one approach* to the situation. Be prepared to offer options with the advantages and disadvantages of each. Don't forget to discuss specific benefits that your client will receive. If possible, give your client some idea of the required time and cost of doing the job. Again, these are just rough estimates, but the client will appreciate even this, and you will make points on preparation.

Do you suggest yourself as a provider of the service? Of course, unless you honestly believe you are not the right one to do the job. (Then you may want to recommend a better-qualified organization. You, of course, run the risk of introducing another firm that could later threaten your present relationship.) But let's take a more positive position and say that you do feel qualified to do an outstanding job. In presenting your credentials, be sure to include your special knowledge of your client's industry, business organization, and other conditions. This will give you an edge that cannot be met by any competition. Include the special talents and background of the people who will work on the job and convey your confidence in them. If possible, establish a sense of urgency, a need for the client to act soon.

Your client may look at you and say, "Let's go." In that case, end the meeting and get started. More likely, he will say he needs to think more about it. If that happens, be patient. You have planted the seed, and after a respectable time, you can raise the issue again.

To summarize, cross-selling services to your existing clients has the greatest potential for bringing in additional business. The selling techniques are the same as those for selling prospective clients, and you have the additional advantages of knowing your client and of your client's knowing you and what you can do.

SKILL-BUILDING TECHNIQUES

Review your client list. Select one client who you believe has a problem or opportunity and who could benefit from receiving additional services you could offer. Collect the information you need for an effective presentation. Contact the client and set up a meeting to present your approach.

Chapter Twelve

Getting
the Edge

You now know most of the skills needed to sell your services. However, these skills are only one element; to outsell your competitors, who may be learning the same or similar skills, you must do more. This last chapter discusses some intangibles that you must deal with effectively if you are to get the very thin edge that spells the difference between winning and losing.

PERSONAL COMMUNICATIONS

How you speak will strongly influence the success of the sale. Effective speaking will not guarantee success, but ineffective speaking will almost surely guarantee failure. A poorly chosen word cannot be pulled back and edited. Many politicians and salespeople have wished they had a second chance after saying something to offend their constituents or customers. Sometimes you cannot think of the right word or phrase to use in an important situation and you choose the wrong words. Nor is a poor selection of words the only danger. Some people unfortunately just do not sound interesting. Either the tone of their voice is boring, the pitch is unpleasant, or they have some habit that turns off the prospect. Whether by choosing the wrong words or by saying them improperly, making a poor impression will jeopardize the sale.

This section reviews some "communications traps" to see what you can do to avoid them. However, before proceeding, let's be clear that we are not suggesting that you completely change your personality or personal style. It is important that you be yourself and that you feel comfortable with what you say and how you say it. All people exhibit some of the potential "sales killers" to a certain degree. Let's see what techniques can be improved or replaced with better ones.

Vocabulary.   How good is your vocabulary? Do you use the same words over and over again? Do you sometimes grope for the right word or phrase in an important situation? These are indications that your vocabulary is limited and holds you back from expressing yourself well. Obviously, you don't need to score 100 percent on the *New York Times* crossword puzzle or consistently string together six-syllable words in a casual conversation. What will work is to begin reading material that both interests you and exposes you to a greater range of words and ideas. When you encounter a word you don't know, look it up. Increase your acquaintance with people who have a wide vocabulary. Not only will they be a good example, they also will be a more receptive audience to your efforts. Check a few of your favorite, frequently used words to be sure they are correct. For example, the word "irregardless" is mentioned in the dictionary, but in parentheses is the phrase: "not generally regarded as good usage." Also, remember to avoid using technical terms with prospects who may not understand them.

Pronunciation.   Any sales presentation is weakened by mispronounced words (for example, "git" for "get," "ath-a-lete" for "athlete"). One grows accustomed to saying words in a particular incorrect way and few except teachers in grade school bother to correct pronunciation because it can prove embarrassing. One way to improve is to record a conversation with another person and play it back. If your ears do not pick up the errors, have a knowledgeable person listen as well. You will probably find, like most of us, that you have only a few weaknesses that you need to concentrate on correcting. However, if your problem is more serious, consider enrolling with a diction instructor.

Do not confuse mispronunciation with a regional accent. Accents from different parts of the country or from other countries not only are acceptable but have a charm of their own. The only time you should be concerned with your accent is when it is so thick that most people outside of your own region have difficulty understanding you.

Jargon.   Jargon is that special language that is unique to a particular industry or business, in this case the accounting profession. Jargon may be expressed as a tax statute, a number of a form or procedure, or a particular business operation. It is used in both writing and speaking.

The problem with jargon is that it is understood only by the enlightened group that uses it regularly. Others who may be present when it is used may feel excluded from the conversation, as happened in this instance:

George and I were having lunch with a new prospect who was considering putting in a new EDP system. We got excited about the options that were available and started throwing expressions around that the prospect was obviously hearing for the first time. Unfortunately, he was either too polite, embarrassed, or intimidated to say anything.

The danger of using jargon with clients and prospects is obvious. If you think you have this problem, monitor your conversations when the "unenlightened" are present.

Clichés.   Everybody uses clichés. Sometimes they express best what we want to say, but often they are too trite and stereotyped to be useful. They may be understood but because of overuse have little impact. Here is a list of common clichés. Cover the right side of the page with your hand and see how many expressions you can finish. You should get all or almost all of them.

1. That's the name of the .... game.
2. Getting to the heart of the .... matter.
3. That's the bottom .... line.
4. Begging the .... issue.

5. Now or .... never.
6. The acid .... test.
7. Above and beyond the .... call of duty.
8. Don't upset the .... apple cart.
9. To be perfectly .... honest.
10. A breath of .... fresh air.
11. To make a long .... story short.
12. Like butting your head .... against the wall.
13. Knock on .... wood.
14. Getting down to brass .... tacks.
15. Don't jump to .... conclusions.
16. Too numerous to .... mention.
17. Without further .... ado.
18. Better late than .... never.
19. Conspicuous by its .... absence.
20. Few and far .... between.

Clichés are not really dangerous, but using them deprives you of the opportunity to be creative in what you say. They are similar to those tired old greetings for which we expect no real answer, like, "What's new?"; "How's tricks?"; "What are you up to?"; "Staying out of trouble?" These expressions are often heard when meeting someone on an elevator for 5 seconds—definitely avoid them when greeting your prospect at a sales meeting.

The best way to avoid clichés and meaningless statements is to be aware of when you use them. Concentrate on using other words or expressions that more closely describe how you feel or what you think at that time.

Slang.   We are all used to slang—hearing it, using it, and in some cases creating it. It usually represents the culture of a particular time and therefore is often short-lived. It can be effective in conversation as long as the other person understands what you are saying. The biggest problem with slang is that it can be misunderstood by someone who is not part of your culture or generation. Also, use of slang often can sound overly casual and can interfere with the seriousness of the dialogue. The guideline on slang is to use it if the occasion fits, but do not get lazy and use it indiscriminately.

Be careful using idioms of your language that may be unfamiliar to prospects of other nationalities. Most foreigners have learned English as part of their formal schooling and for the most part handle it well. However, avoid any idioms that might be misunderstood. That is a

pretty reasonable request considering that most of us are not prepared to converse in any language other than our own.

Profanity.   In a word—*Don't!* Granted, you may be a very earthy
person who says what you mean and believes a few four-letter words
can't hurt anyone, and granted, there are prospects who feel the
same way. But why take a chance on offending someone or
degrading your service? If the prospect wants to throw around a few
choice explicit words, fine. Save yours for the time, place, and people
where you cannot get hurt.

Humor.   Is there a place for humor in the sales presentation? Of
course. An opportunity to enjoy a laugh with the prospect can lighten
the atmosphere and pave the way for freer conversation. The most
effective humor usually happens spontaneously; neither party plans
it or expects it. How about jokes or humorous anecdotes? OK, but
there are a few guidelines. First, does your prospect appreciate
hearing them? It might be better to get to know her before you share
that sidesplitter you heard at the office. Are you pretty good at telling
jokes, or do you have a poor memory and a talent for lousing up the
punch line? If being humorous is not among your best attributes,
don't practice on the prospect. On the other hand, if you are
comfortable and good in that role and the situation looks right, take
advantage of it. However, be careful that your stories are not too long
and are not in poor taste, and do not take cheap shots at ethnic
groups. Before I take away all your fun, you might consider yourself
as a target of humor—Jack Benny made a few million dollars that way
and was pretty well-liked too.

Your Voice.   It is important to know how your voice sounds to
others. Not everyone can be blessed with a rich-timbred voice that
enchants those around them. In fact, such a voice is a rarity that
seems to be found mostly in stage actors and anchorpeople on the late
evening news. A voice that is monotone, shrill, lacking in contrast, or
otherwise unpleasant to hear can be a definite liability in selling.
Equally negative is the tempo that sounds like either a machine gun
or a sleep-inducing drone.

   If you qualify for one of these conditions, do not despair. You may
never develop the melodious tones you would love to have, but you
can improve. Diction and voice instructors can help you make a

significant difference in how you sound and in how you feel about your voice. At a reasonable cost they will diagnose your problem and give you a number of exercises and techniques to get you closer to your goals. As with any consultant, find one that has had success in treating your particular condition.

ORGANIZING YOUR SELLING TIME

As mentioned earlier, CPAs and other professionals often claim that they have difficulty finding the time to sell because it is a function added to other things they must do. This statement is only partially accurate: It *is* an additional function for many of you, but forget about *finding* the time to sell. There is no more time; 24 hours a day is all you get, and you are probably using every hour of it now. What you need to do is not to find time but to *make* time to sell. One colleague put it this way:

There is never enough time, but I have set my priorities and I get done what is most important. For me, getting new business is right at the top. I've heard some say, "Take away some of my workload and I'll spend more time selling." I don't buy that. If you want to sell, you'll find a way to make time for it and still get your other jobs done. You may have to work faster and not do such a detailed job, or you may have to delegate more, but nobody's going to reduce your workload for you.

Clearly, making time for selling becomes a tradeoff, trading off one job for another, and you may have noticed how easy it is to trade off a job you don't like for one you do like. There is some validity for that reasoning as indicated here:

One guy can't do everything. I can't, mainly because I'm not inter-ested in everything. I can't do a good job with something that doesn't interest me. So I get involved in something I like and do well and leave the other jobs to other people. One thing I do like is selling new business and expanding business for existing clients. I spend a lot of time with that.

However, the nature of your business requires that several jobs must get done, and that requires planning and managing your time. Most of you have probably either attended a time management semi-nar or read a book on the subject, but it might be interesting to see how others plan for the selling role. One CPA interviewed does the following:

I spend a good deal of time planning what I've got to do. I plan on the train, on planes, and at home. I like to plan at least 6 months in advance. I have some pretty specific goals I want to accomplish in the next 3 years, and I can't do it without careful planning and sticking to that plan. I'm after that 3-year goal, and bringing in new business is a big part of that goal. How do I get everything done? I don't, but that's the way it is. I delegate like hell and take my chances.

Sometimes you can do some innovative things in planning your time to accomplish your selling goals, but be prepared to get some raised eyebrows from others, as does this CPA:

How do I plan my time? Mostly I'm out with clients and prospects. I spend very little time in the office, and I get a lot of flak from my partners, but I want to know what is happening with my clients, and not just what deals with the audit. I want to know what's happening in their business, what problems they're having. I'm in the office by 6:30 or 7:00 a.m. By 8:30 I've checked my mail, picked up my phone calls, and cleaned up some old work, and I'm on my way. See this briefcase? There's about 2 or 3 hours of work for the _____ Company. Instead of doing it in my office, I'll do it out there. It gets done more quickly, the client sees it as a service call, and I get a chance to nose around for problems and potential business. In a sense I'm combining client retention and marketing in the same visit.

This chapter does not go into great detail on the principles of planning, but a list of a few guidelines will help if you are serious about making selling a part of your career.

1. Make a conscious decision to set aside a certain number of hours each month for selling. Announce your plan to at least one other person; this will help you to stay committed to your plan.
2. Review your time reports to determine where and how you are spending your time. Decide which of these activities could be dropped, reduced, or delegated. These are the hours that will be replaced with selling. This may be a painful exercise, because giving up the old comfortable activities is difficult, but it's like pulling off a bandage—once it's off, the pain is gone.
3. Make a list of desirable prospects and identify the decision makers and powers of influence. These may be people you've known for a while, have just met, or would like to meet.
4. Narrow the list down to two or three hot prospects, ones you think

you have a fair chance of getting. Don't make your task seem impossible by tackling too many prospects at one time.

5. Do some preliminary research using the 4-P formula discussed in Chapter 5. If possible, enlist the help of a staff person to help with this research. It will save you some time.

6. Determine the best way to contact your prospects. For those you know or have just met, consider calling them to discuss a matter of interest to them. For those people you would like to meet, try to find out where they spend their time (see Chapter 3) so that you can plan to be there or have someone who knows them introduce you to them.

7. If you are to make the contact at a social function, pencil it into your notebook and *don't cancel* unless you have a better selling opportunity. If you want to arrange a personal meeting with the prospect, select several open dates in your calendar. Pick up the phone and agree on a date. Don't hang up until you have agreement on a meeting.

8. Use the contact record (see Chapter 5, last page) for each prospect you plan to meet with. Avoid the temptation of filling out a lot of prospect records for prospects you are not now calling on. You don't want to be in the office doing clerical work when you should be out selling. Keep a record of the results of each phone call, meeting, or other contact you have with the prospect.

9. At the end of the month, compare the time you actually spent on selling to the time you planned to spend. If it is as much or greater than what you planned, then you have made a successful transition—you not only have tried something new, you have let go of something old.

These are not very tough guidelines, but they will get you started and keep you on track.

CONSIDERING YOUR PERSONAL TIME

For most CPAs, taking on more work is not a new situation. You are used to taking on another job, and somehow you always seem to be able to handle it. Yet selling does have certain unique time requirements that may cause you to make some changes. Consider this CPA's story:

I always thought I led a pretty full life. I usually worked from about 8:00 in the morning to 6:00 or 7:00 at night. I put in at least one night a week on some professional activity. Other nights I spent with my family or worked in my shop in my basement. I enjoy making or repairing furniture, nothing elaborate. On the weekend I usually golfed one day with some good friends. When I decided to really get involved in the selling activity, I found I needed to devote more after-hours time to meeting prospects. I decided not to take away any time from my family. So, I dropped my professional activity night as it was mostly technical subjects for which I had decreasing interest. I cut out one night of my shop work and on the weekend began to make some golf dates with prospects. My golf friends kidded me about that, but they understood.

So, you may find that you will have to give up or rearrange some of your personal activities. That is the price you have to pay to do the job right.

Unfortunately, because selling is often best done after the regular work day, it can conflict with the time you normally spend with your family. If that occurs, you had better sit down and talk about it with your spouse or children, as did this CPA:

When we were first married, my wife and I discussed my job. She knew I would be putting in long hours, especially during the tax season, and that was all right. We both believed that as I advanced in the firm the long hours would decrease, but somehow that never happened. There was always a new responsibility that took time. When I decided to seriously get involved in selling and looked at the time requirements, I knew I had a problem. My wife and I talked about it and, in the course of our discussion, reviewed our lifestyle and what she wanted for herself and the children. In short, we set new priorities which caused me to drop some of my work activities. But I kept my selling role because it was important for me and it was what I wanted to do.

Your spouse can be a source of support for your new role and can sometimes be a strong ally in accomplishing your goals. But, you have to be willing to talk about your business with your spouse. Some accountants think that their wives or husbands are not interested in their work. That may be true for the more technical aspects of your job, but a selling opportunity can be very exciting and of interest to your mate, so share your day just the way your spouse shares his or her day with you. One CPA describes his wife's role this way:

I spend a lot of evenings trying to bring in business, but a lot of that time is entertaining a prospect and his wife. Of course my wife is present. We do this regularly, so I really consider her to be an active participant. She's interested in this part of the business. She enjoys doing it, and we have something worthwhile to share and talk about. I know a lot of wives resent their husbands' being away from home in the evenings, and I think it's because they are not part of what's happening. They feel excluded.

In some cases, a person's spouse not only has become interested in the selling activity but also has actually been instrumental in bringing in new business. If your spouse is in business, she or he may come in contact with other businesspeople in their fields who have a need for your help. Or your spouse may be very involved in community activities. In either case, you should familiarize your spouse with what your firm offers and, even more important, encourage him or her to tactfully probe for opportunities and problems when talking to their business associates and friends. With that information you could be into your next selling step.

Let us review. First, commit to a certain number of selling hours. Then, examine how you are presently spending your time. Rid yourself of work that is less important or can be done by others to allow you to fit in the selling time. Pick a few hot prospects, call them, and keep a record of your meetings. At the end of the month, audit your performance, not so much to see what you have sold but to see if you have stuck to your plan.

Examine the impact of selling on your personal and family life. Work out any conflicts with those that may be affected. Try to enlist, at the very least, the moral support of those who are close to you. If you are fortunate enough to have someone who wants to actively help you sell, by all means, take advantage of that opportunity.

DEVELOPING OTHER SKILLS AND QUALITIES

Like an artist, a musician, or a professional athlete, you must now hone your skills so that you can acquire the advantage over all the others who are trying to do the same thing. You must also recognize the need to develop certain attitudes and other personal qualities that not only will give you an edge but also will sustain you in difficult times such as described by this consultant:

When I first started to really get serious about selling, I began like a house on fire. I brought in four new clients in 4 months. Everything I did seemed to go right. Then I began to lose a few. I couldn't understand why. I was doing everything I had learned and had succeeded with previously, yet it was not working. I began to get discouraged and gradually looked for fewer selling opportunities. This, of course, further reduced my sales results, and I felt even worse. It became a vicious cycle.

You do not have to be a CPA to go through that experience. Countless thousands of salespeople in hundreds of industries have found in a relatively short time that selling is tough, that the competition is always looking to move in, and that prospects can be very demanding and stubborn. Like the law of nature, only the fittest survive. Those who do survive and sometimes flourish have followed a plan for constantly improving their skills and learning to deal with adversity.

Let's look first at the skills you need to develop.

- *Know your own services and products and what they can do for your prospects.* Learn about those services that are planned for the future but have not yet been offered to your clients.
- *Develop your communication skills, particularly your ability to speak in public before larger groups.* If necessary, take a speaking course to become comfortable and proficient. Every city has some type of speaking course. The longer ones, like the Dale Carnegie course, have the advantage of giving you sufficient time to practice in a climate of support.
- *Learn more about selling.* The most successful salespeople never stop learning, trying to acquire one more skill that will give them an edge over their competition. Take sales seminars that deal with the kind of selling that is appropriate for professional services. Read books on the subject, and don't forget to speak to successful salespeople in other industries. Have lunch with your clients' top salespeople and get a few tips from them. Salespeople love to talk and share their successes.
- *Become adept at remembering names.* Most people remember names so poorly that the few who do it well really stand out. Actually there is no big mystery to it; it's a matter of learning a few easy techniques and making the effort. A number of good books explain how to develop these various methods. If you want more practice, attend a short course on the subject. Your local school probably gives such a course.
- *Expand your reading to include a wider scope of business subjects.* This will give you more to discuss with prospects than just your ac-

counting, audit, or tax expertise. If you have difficulty selecting the appropriate books, check with your local librarian for suggestions. These people are usually very well-informed and glad to help.

Those are a few skills that are worth improving. Now let's look at some of the personal qualities that you will need to master if you are to be consistently successful at selling your services. These qualities are less tangible than the skills discussed and therefore you may find developing them a little difficult at first.

Be Enthusiastic.   Make increased enthusiasm a major part of your life. This includes being enthusiastic about your firm, your services, and your role in selling. Often the difference in success between two people with the same capability and skills is that one has more enthusiasm. Don't be loud, jump all over the place, or otherwise make yourself look foolish, but do feel good about your career, yourself, and life in general. When you can do this, your enthusiasm will emerge as a powerful positive impression on others. If you are still not sure what we mean, think of some other activity in your life that turns you on, that you love to do or talk about—that's the feeling you want to generate toward selling.

Give Yourself Pep Talks.   What! Is this guy crazy? Does he want me to talk to myself? Yes! Not in front of a crowd of people, although that seems to work very well for athletes as they get ready to start a contest. What you need to do just before you enter the prospect's office or wherever you are going to meet is to literally give yourself a quiet or, at the very least, a silent pep talk. Tell yourself all the reasons you are going to succeed, reasons like: you know your service inside out, you've done your homework and have a good idea of what the prospect needs, you're sure you can help him, you belong to a great firm that is in back of you, and you are definitely going to make this sale. This exercise doesn't cost you a cent, and the benefits are pretty obvious: you will replace negative thoughts with positive ones, every part of your body will be charged with positive excitement, and you will carry a glow of confidence that the prospect can't help but notice and appreciate. If you are still not sold on pep talks, talk to top salespeople and other outstanding performers in business and other fields who have to regularly prepare for high-pressure situations.

Keep the Faith. If you are going to seriously practice the art of selling, unfortunately, you are sometimes going to be rebuffed, put off, rejected, insulted, and otherwise put in a position where you are not going to feel very good. And, you will occasionally fail. At these times you will feel discouraged and ready to chuck it all to become a full-time auditor or tax preparer. Who needs this abuse? You do! No kidding—if you want to become the very best, and why not, then you need to go through this experience. Each time you are rejected, you will become a little tougher and better prepared to handle it next time; each time you fail you will learn something to do or not to do. This is a process of maturation not unlike what you went through to become an excellent accountant or consultant.

Specifically, what do you need to do to keep the faith? First, prepare yourself to experience occasional rejection and failure. Then, after a respectable but brief mourning period, move into a positive track. Think of all the things you have got going for you: your knowledge, your experience, your skills, your personality, and most of all, your past successes. Recall a moment of triumph, a sale that you made that gave you a great feeling. Relive that experience just the way it happened. You'll find the depressed feeling gradually fading and being replaced with a feeling of pride and confidence. Then give yourself a quick pep talk (Remember?) and start planning your next selling strategy. If you want to find out more about this important subject, read some of the inspiring books of Norman Vincent Peale. If you have read them before, they may now have new meaning for you.

YOUR COMMITMENT

Selling is a commitment. You have made a few commitments in your life: perhaps to a marriage, a job, a friendship, or a particular interest. In that commitment, you basically made a decision to make something important in your life work. You were willing to give it time, effort, and, perhaps most important, the chance to succeed, which often meant overcoming obstacles, disappointments, and setbacks. So it is with selling. You need to make a personal commitment to making it work. You know now what you have to do and how to do it. Get a couple of bruises; strike out a couple of times. That's OK. Nobody bats a thousand. But if you want to score big, you have to get into the game, so get out there and give it a try. Good luck!

SKILL-BUILDING TECHNIQUES

Write out your selling goals below for the next 12 months. Make them specific as to names and numbers. Include activities you wish to become involved in, contacts you plan to make, and, of course, sales you want to make. Aim a little higher than you realistically think you can achieve. A little stretching never hurt anyone.

Then, write down some good reasons why you are going to succeed. Think back over your career and personal life; list the personal qualities you've got going for you that will help you succeed, qualities like enthusiasm, perseverance, the desire to be among the best. This is not the time to be modest. This is the time to gather all your resources for a tough challenge and then take charge and move ahead!

SELLING GOALS FOR NEXT 12 MONTHS

1. My selling goals are:

2. I am going to succeed because:

Index

About the Author

Charles Goldsmith has a unique combination of business background and sales experience that is ideal for this book, having been an accountant, a consultant, a salesman, and an instructor of selling and public speaking. He understands the accounting profession, knows how to sell, and can show others how to do it.

As coordinator of management development for the international accounting and financial services firm of Deloitte, Haskins & Sells, Dr. Goldsmith participates in preparing proposals and making presentations to prospective clients. He also develops and teaches courses and seminars designed to improve the selling and communication skills of CPAs and consultants. The programs he has developed have been adopted in countries around the world.

Previously, Dr. Goldsmith held management positions with Dun & Bradstreet and the Metropolitan Life Insurance Company and was director of sales development for the Swiss watch industry. A licensed Dale Carnegie instructor, he holds a master's degree in accounting and obtained his Ph.D. at New York University.